W9-CNY-925

DISCARDED
UNIVERSITY OF WINNIPEG
LIBRARY
515 Portage Avenue
Winnipeg, Manitoba R3B 2E9

BURNS & HIS POETRY

Robert Burns

BURNS & HIS POETRY

BY

H. A. KELLOW M.A.

KENNIKAT PRESS
Port Washington, N. Y./London

BURNS & HIS POETRY

First published in 1911
Reissued in 1970 by Kennikat Press
Library of Congress Catalog Card No: 70-105798
ISBN 0-8046-1024-X

Manufactured by Taylor Publishing Company Dallas, Texas

GENERAL PREFACE

A GLANCE through the pages of this little book will suffice to disclose the general plan of the series of which it forms a part. Only a few words of explanation, therefore, will be necessary.

The point of departure is the undeniable fact that with the vast majority of young students of literature a living interest in the work of any poet can best be aroused, and an intelligent appreciation of it secured, when it is immediately associated with the character and career of the poet himself. The cases are indeed few and far between in which much fresh light will not be thrown upon a poem by some knowledge of the personality of the writer, while it will often be found that the most direct—perhaps even the only—way to the heart of its meaning lies through a consideration of the circumstances in which it had its birth. The purely æsthetic critic may possibly object that a poem should be regarded simply as a self-contained and detached piece of art, having no personal affiliations or bearings. Of the validity of this as an abstract principle nothing need now be said. The fact remains that, in the earlier stages of study at any rate, poetry is most valued and loved when it is made to seem most human and vital; and the human and vital interest of poetry can be most surely brought home to the reader by the biographical method of interpretation.

This is to some extent recognised by writers of histories and text-books of literature, and by editors of selections from the works of our poets; for place is always given by them to a certain amount of biographical material. But in the histories and text-books the biography of a given writer stands by itself, and his work has to be sought elsewhere, the student being left to make the connection for himself; while even in our current editions of selections there is little systematic attempt to link biography, step by step, with production.

This brings us at once to the chief purpose of the present series. In this, biography and production will be considered together and in intimate association. In other words, an endeavour will be made to interest the reader in the lives and personalities of the poets dealt with, and at the same time to use biography as an introduction and key to their writings.

Each volume will therefore contain the life-story of the poet who forms its subject. In this attention will be specially directed to his personality as it expressed itself in his poetry, and to the influences and conditions which counted most as formative factors in the growth of his genius. This biographical study will be used as a setting for a selection, as large as space will permit, of his representative poems. Such poems, where possible, will be reproduced in full, and care will be taken to bring out their connection with his character, his circumstances, and the movement of his mind. Then, in addition, so much more general literary criticism will be incorporated as may seem to be needed to supplement the biographical material, and to exhibit both the essential qualities and the historical importance of his work.

It is believed that the plan thus pursued is substantially in the nature of a new departure, and that the volumes of this series, constituting as they will an introduction to the study of some of our greatest poets, will be found useful to teachers and students of literature, and no less to the general lover of English poetry.

WILLIAM HENRY HUDSON

POEMS QUOTED IN WHOLE OR IN PART

PAGE

Handsome Nell 19
Mary Morison 27
The Epistle to Davie 33
Halloween 39
To a Mouse 40
To a Mountain Daisy 43
The Farmer's Salutation to his Auld Mare 45
The Cotter's Saturday Night 46
Holy Willie's Prayer 55
Epistle to William Simson 56
To the Unco Guid 57
Farewell to the Banks of Ayr 64
A Bard's Epitaph 65
Epistle to a Young Friend 67
The Twa Brigs 71
The Lass o' Ballochmyle 72
Lines on Meeting with Lord Daer 74
Of a' the Airts the Wind can blaw 88
Auld Lang Syne 91
The Banks of Nith 92
The Banks o' Doon 92
Afton Water 93
Willie brew'd a Peck o' Maut 95
To Mary in Heaven 96
Tam o' Shanter 99
A Man's a Man for a' That 112
A Red, Red Rose 119
Ae Fond Kiss 120
When I think on the Happy Days 120
O, wert thou in the Cauld Blast 121

BIBLIOGRAPHY

The following list contains the titles of a few books and essays which may be specially recommended for the further study of Burns and his work :

Lockhart, J. G. : " Life of Burns."

Shairp, J. C. : " Burns " (English Men of Letters).

Blackie, J. S. : " Burns " (Great Writers).

Carlyle, T. : " Burns " (in "Critical and Miscellaneous Essays," vol. ii.).

Henley and Henderson : " The Poetry of Robert Burns " (the best text).

Note.—Blackie's volume in the " Great Writers " series contains a very full bibliography.

BURNS AND HIS POETRY

ROBERT BURNS, lawful son of William Burnes, in Alloway, and Agnes Brown, his spouse, was born January 25, 1759: baptized by Mr. William Dalrymple. Witnesses, John Tennant and James Young." The birth, parentage, and christening of the greatest Scottish poet are thus officially recorded in the church registers of the parish of Ayr and Alloway Respectable witnesses, officiating clergyman, mother, father, and child —how many similar groups of individuals had their names inscribed in the session books of the Kirk of Scotland for that year! And how many names still lie there, hidden in decent obscurity, alms for oblivion! In all such baptismal ceremonies the child must cut the greatest figure: he is the great potentiality: what he is to become no one can tell. It is improbable that John Tennant and James Young, the witnesses of this genuinely notable event, had even a glimmering of the true importance of the occasion. Humble bystanders at his first sacrament, they could not be expected to realise the future greatness of their honest neighbour's bairn and to conceive of the genius that lay dormant within his puny frame. Stark truth it is that in the baptismal scene which the official entry coniures to the imagination the presiding genius is not the minister—reverend doctor though he be—and not the parent, but the child, Robert Burns.

The world is not content to read the family history of a great man solely from his birth certificate. The ancestry of the poet has therefore been the subject of diligent inquiry. Burns himself seems to have had the vaguest notions of his lineage, but it can now be traced with certainty on the father's side for five, and on the mother's side for three generations. Agnes Brown, the mother of Burns, was the daughter of one Gilbert Brown, farmer at Craigenton, in Kirkoswald Parish, Ayrshire. Her grandfather was John Brown, also a farmer at Craigenton. The Browns appear to have been Covenanters, and the poet believed that the famous John Brown of Priesthill, the stubborn Presbyterian who was shot by Claverhouse's troopers in 1685, belonged to his mother's family. Seizing upon this fact, some writers have attributed to the influence of heredity a certain dourness of disposition and rebellious spirit towards authority which Burns undoubtedly evinced. But this is altogether fanciful, and is discounted by the fact that on the paternal side the poet's ancestors were perfervid Royalists, and Jacobites to boot. Writing to Dr. John Moore, the physician and novelist, on August 2, 1787, Burns asserted that his forefathers rented land of the famous, noble Keiths of Marshal (the Earls Marischal), and had the honour to share their fate. The distinguished Scottish house of Keith forfeited their title and estates in the Fifteen, and their adherents, among whom was the poet's grandfather, were plundered and driven out. This grandfather, Robert Burnes, rented a poor farm near Stonehaven, Kincardineshire. He was unable to support his large family of ten children on this farm, and although the yearly rent was only £10 8s. 4d. sterling, he fell into arrears, and latterly was compelled to quit his holding. His third son, William Burnes, born in 1721, determined to try his fortune in the south, and, after a spell of work as a gardener in Edinburgh, migrated to Ayrshire in 1750. At Alloway he set up as a nurseryman or market-gardener, leasing seven acres of land for that purpose. On December 15, 1757, he married Agnes Brown, and they forthwith took up house in a clay cottage which he had built with his own hands. In this cottage their famous son, Robert Burns, the poet, was born. From all this it will appear that Burns was descended from rather a poverty-stricken tenant-farmer stock, and that, as he himself phrased it, he "was born a very poor man's son."

Although Burns's mother was never able to write even her name, her husband was a man of some education. He could both read and write ; and in those days that was indeed an accomplishment for a person of his class. But, after all, these are almost mechanical attainments, and they must be regarded as the least noteworthy of William Burnes's claims to distinction. His strong intellect, his high character, his very speech marked him out as superior to his neighbours. A devout man, much conversant with the speculative theology engendered by the brooding Calvinism of the age, he had high ideals of family life, and both by precept and example took care to lead his children in the path of virtue. He exerted himself as their instructor, with the result that in after years his family were always regarded as the most book-learned in the parish. To him the poet owed most of his early education. In 1765, when Robert was in his sixth year, the father cast about to procure outside assistance in this task. In the month of March he interviewed, at Ayr, a young teacher named John Murdoch, and in the May following he took the lead in establishing Murdoch at Alloway, being one of five who guaranteed to board the teacher by turns and to make up a certain salary for him should the fees prove insufficient. At a time when a cotter, without incurring disgrace or even censure, might have neglected altogether the formal education of his offspring, it is remarkable that William Burnes should be found making these uncommon exertions on behalf of his family.

But the best that William Burnes could afford seems now poor indeed. John Murdoch was a raw lad of eighteen when he began to teach the little school at Alloway. His attainments in after life were considerable ; but at this period he certainly did not far surpass

William Burnes in scholarship. The latter acted as co-instructor to his own boys while they were under Murdoch's charge, and the result was that between the two preceptors the lads made excellent progress. "Though I cost the schoolmaster some thrashings," wrote Robert in 1787, in an autobiographical letter to Dr. Moore, "I made an excellent English scholar ; and against the years of ten or eleven, I was absolutely a critic in substantives, verbs, and particles." This proficiency in grammar must be attributed directly to Murdoch, and fortunately he has left an interesting account of how it was attained. Thirty-three years after he began his work at Alloway he thus described his early teaching experiences : "Robert and his younger brother, Gilbert, had been grounded a little in English before they were put under my care. They both made a rapid progress in reading, and a tolerable progress in writing. In reading, dividing words into syllables by rule, spelling without book, parsing sentences, &c., Robert and Gilbert were generally at the upper end of the class, even when ranged with boys far their seniors. The books most commonly used in the school were the 'Spelling Book,' the New Testament, the Bible, Masson's 'Collection of Prose and Verse,' and Fisher's 'English Grammar.' They committed to memory the hymns and other poems of that collection with uncommon facility. This facility was partly owing to the method pursued by their father and me in instructing them, which was, to make them thoroughly acquainted with the meaning of every word in each sentence that was to be committed to memory. As soon as they were capable of it, I taught them to turn verse into its natural prose order; sometimes to substitute synonymous expressions for poetical words, and to supply all the ellipses."

It is noteworthy that the early education of Burns was almost exclusively literary. His weakness in handwriting was, some years afterwards, remedied at the parish school of Dalrymple which he and Gilbert attended, week about, for a quarter. Burns certainly did not count it a baseness to write fair. He always took great pride in his correspondence, and the manuscripts of his poems are invariably written in a neat, legible hand. The instruction in arithmetic provided by Murdoch was probably also defective. But as an English teacher Murdoch undoubtedly excelled, and in English Burns proved himself an apt pupil. He soon gained fluency and correctness of expression, and thus laid the foundation for that skill in conversation for which he was afterwards famous. His memory was from the very first remarkably retentive: he had almost all the New Testament by heart. The first prose piece in which he took particular pleasure was "The Vision of Mirza"; the earliest verse, Addison's hymn beginning "How are Thy servants blest, O Lord." These he found in his school reader. The first reading that he did outside school hours was "The Life of Hannibal," lent him by

Murdoch, and "The History of Sir William Wallace," lent by a friendly blacksmith. The former stirred him to a boyish enthusiasm for a soldier's life; the latter endowed him with the perfervid patriotism peculiar to the Scot.

If these books were read at Alloway, Burns was not then eight years old. What modern child of that age finds pleasure in Addison's "Vision of Mirza"? But it is more probable that, precocious as Burns undoubtedly was, these books were read at Mount Oliphant, a poor upland farm of seventy acres in the parish of Ayr, to which William Burnes removed in 1766. Mount Oliphant lay two miles distant from Alloway, and for a time Robert and Gilbert trudged that long road to the school. Murdoch records that their attendance became irregular and that latterly they ceased coming altogether. The whole time that Robert attended cannot have been much more than two years. Other causes forced Murdoch to give up his little school, but before leaving Alloway he visited Mount Oliphant, and from his small store of books he gave Robert, as a parting present, an English Grammar, and purposed giving him a copy of "Titus Andronicus" also. The teacher spent some of the time reading portions of this sordid play to the family circle, and Robert, it is recorded, burst into tears at the treatment of the heroine and refused to accept the present of such a horrible book. William Burnes chid his son for this ingratitude, but Murdoch, perhaps more pleased than otherwise at the display of sensibility, left in its stead a comedy translated from the French, entitled "The School for Love." Burns was then between nine and ten years of age, and to a boy of so ardent a temperament and imagination the work of the farm, which he was now called upon to share, must have been very uncongenial. Burns ever afterwards spoke of this period with bitterness of soul. His father had commenced farming on borrowed capital, and from the start he was unfortunate. He lost some of his cattle by accidents and disease, and the very soil he tilled was the poorest ever cultivated. Strict economy was needed, and the family had to subsist on the hardest fare. Nevertheless William Burnes did what he could for the education of his family. When the labours of the day were over he instructed his children himself. His eldest son mentions the fact that the whole Burns household used to practise arithmetic in the long winter evenings, a candle being set in their midst. The father did his best to procure books for his elder boys, and amongst those which Robert devoured were "Pamela," "Peregrine Pickle," a volume of "English History," a collection of "English Songs," "The Edinburgh Magazine" for 1772, Pope's "Works," and certain pieces of poetry such as were then hawked through the country or sold at fairs at a penny each. These last consisted of ballads and songs—some of distinct literary value—and played no small part in the training of the poet. Thus, although

Burns had little regular schooling, he was in the way of acquiring a fair education. Moreover in 1773 he was sent to Ayr to study under Murdoch for a few weeks in order that he should revise his grammar and be better qualified to instruct his brothers and sisters at home. But even this chance of improvement was jeopardised; he had been at Ayr only one week when he was recalled to assist in the harvest. Afterwards he was allowed to go back for two weeks. Judged by modern standards, a total of three weeks' instruction—broken in upon at that—seems ridiculously small; but to a lad of the keenness, intelligence, and extraordinary gifts of Burns it proved very valuable.

When he was summoned from Ayr to the harvest-field it happened that the partner of his labours was a "bonnie, sweet, sonsie lass" named Nelly Kilpatrick, a young girl of about his own age. As she worked she sang a song which had been composed by a neighbouring country lad, and Burns in emulation made up a song about the singer. Thus was his first poem born.

HANDSOME NELL

O, once I lov'd a bonnie lass,
  Aye, and I love her still!
And whilst that virtue warms my breast
  I'll love my handsome Nell.

As bonnie lasses I hae seen,
  And mony full as braw,

But for a modest gracefu' mien
  The like I never saw.

A bonnie lass, I will confess,
  Is pleasant to the e'e ;
But, without some better qualities,
  She's no a lass for me.

But Nelly's looks are blithe and sweet,
  And, what is best of a',
Her reputation is complete,
  And fair without a flaw.

She dresses aye sae clean and neat,
  Both decent and genteel :
And, then there's something in her gait
  Gars ony dress look weel.

A gaudy dress and gentle air
  May slightly touch the heart ;
But it's innocence and modesty
  That polishes the dart.

'Tis this in Nelly pleases me,
  'Tis this enchants my soul !
For absolutely in my breast
  She reigns without control.

Burns is said to have written this poem in 1773—that is, when he was in his fifteenth summer. There is no remarkable precocity here. Pope wrote an ode on "Solitude" before he was twelve ; at fourteen he made a verse translation of the "Thebais" ; at sixteen he produced his "Pastorals." When fifteen

Milton translated two Psalms which he afterwards thought worthy of publication. Abraham Cowley wrote "Pyramus and Thisbe" when he was ten, and actually published a volume of poetry when he was fifteen. Many such early instances, not only of power of language but of comprehension of things, might be culled from literary history. Even in the present age the schools have smart boys able to write passable verse. Nevertheless the first work of a great poet must always be scanned with interest. The poem, as it stands, may not be the original version, for Burns certainly was at work on it ten years later than 1773. How far it was then retouched it is impossible to say: probably very little. The poet himself has criticised it adversely; he thinks it puerile and silly: but many critics pretend to see in it the promise and potency of future greatness. It is certainly not silly; but its lack of passion is evidence of its puerility. To the student of Burns's poetry its interest lies in its form—that of the song; its theme—love; and its inspiration—music.

Robert had left Ayr a schoolboy: he returned a poet. And this fact doubtless explains the fierce enthusiasm with which he attacked his studies. His teacher marvelled at it: "He was now with me day and night, in school, at all meals, and in all my walks. At the end of one week I told him that as he was now pretty much master of the parts of speech, I should like to teach him something of French. Robert was glad to hear of the proposal, and immediately we attacked the French with great courage. He was hourly laying in a stock of words and even of phrases. At the end of our second week of the study of French we began to read a little of 'The Adventures of Telemachus' in Fénelon's own words." This book and a dictionary Robert took back to Mount Oliphant, and in a little while, with their assistance, he acquired such a knowledge of the language as to read and understand any French prose. Elated with his success and thirsting for more knowledge, he purchased a Latin grammar, but, finding it dry and uninteresting, gave it up in disgust. In his scanty leisure he read everything that came his way, and when he had nothing fresh to read he read and re-read the old books. On the farm he had to do the work of a grown man, for his father could not afford hired help. There is some evidence that Robert resented the way in which his labour was exploited. William Burnes, though a just, was also a hard man, and it is probable that there was an occasional conflict of wills between father and son. And while it is recognised that the father acted in the best interests of all his family, yet it seems hard that a lad, ambitious to be a scholar, should have to toil and moil in all the drudgery of farm work. However, it had to be done, and two years passed in sore labour before the young student had again the chance of following the natural bent of his mind.

In his seventeenth year Burns attended a school at Kirkoswald, and there he took lessons in arithmetic, dialling, and land-surveying. This was an excellent training for a farmer with aspirations, but the company of young ardent spirits with whom he was thrown into contact probably did more for him than did the mathematical instruction of the pedagogue. Burns was eager to compete against his fellows, and entered with zest into all manner of contests. In conversation, in disputations, and in the intellectual combats generally he proved his prowess, but in the ordinary sports and pastimes he did not distinguish himself. Even at this time his frame had taken the ploughman set: he was a strong, slow-moving, cumbrous sort of person. The impress of those early years of premature toil at Mount Oliphant could never be effaced. Meanwhile his heart was young, and when he was introduced to fair Peggy Thomson he must needs celebrate the occasion with song. The song in honour of Peggy, so far as is known, is his second attempt at verse. It is said that he composed several other songs while at Kirkoswald, but nothing can be assigned with certainty to this period. He carefully studied the art of prose-writing, and soon began to take pride in his ability to turn out a touching "billet-doux."

The summer which Burns spent at Kirkoswald was one of the great formative periods of his life. It gave him a turn for sociability and took him out of himself. Before he went he was brooding, distant, suspicious, uncompanionable: when he returned he was hail-fellow-well-met with acquaintances, he possessed great facility of address, and in an argument he had a tongue with a tang. In the years immediately succeeding his sojourn at Kirkoswald he even blossomed forth as a dandy. He wore the only tied hair in the parish of Tarbolton, his plaid was always wrapped round him in a distinctive manner, and his whole bearing bespoke the man of originality and genius. He enlarged his reading considerably, and began to betray a taste for the polemical literature of religion and philosophy. At Tarbolton he was accustomed to meet with kindred spirits, and in order that they might have some definite and formal organisation he founded the Bachelors' Club, a kind of debating society. He drew up its constitution, presided over its meetings, and carefully prepared the speeches which he delivered there. This in itself was an admirable training for him, though the lofty and philosophic opinions expressed at these meetings showed a peculiarly unworldly outlook on life.

That Burns was enabled to do all these things indicates some betterment in the family fortunes. In 1777 William Burnes had removed from Mount Oliphant and had entered on the tenancy of another farm, Lochlea; and the change seems at first to have put him in possession of some needful cash. Robert and Gilbert now received wages for their labour, being paid at the rate of seven pounds per annum apiece. In addition their father gave them, as a private venture, the use of certain land in return for a fixed rent, in order to grow flax, then a profitable crop in the West of Scotland, but now no longer grown. Robert at this time had a mind to set up house, and had high hopes of making money enough to support a wife. When about twenty-two he had fallen in love with one Ellison Begbie, the daughter of a farmer in the district. Naturally she inspired him to write something in her honour, and he wrote both prose and verse to her. In a song of similes, her charms are catalogued after the usual fashion of young poets in love. This production is, on the whole, artificial ; many of the similes are the stock-in-trade of all versifiers, and where Burns strikes out an original one it is not always with happy effect. More remarkable than the verse are the letters which he wrote to Ellison. The correspondence shows that already Burns had developed great facility of expression and an extraordinary range of construction and vocabulary. It is doubtful whether the servant girl thoroughly understood the compositions of the young farmer, for they are philosophical disquisitions rather than love-letters. This is not strange when it is understood that in almost every letter Burns had a definite model in front of him, taken from a collection of the letters by the wits of Queen Anne's reign. Soulful protestations of love cannot be based upon "a complete letter-writer." Nevertheless the courtship proceeded smoothly enough for some time, and Burns prudently determined to learn the art of flax-dressing so that he would reap a greater profit from the flax grown on the farm. He made all arrangements to proceed to the town of Irvine for this purpose, but just prior to his leaving Lochlea fate dealt him a cruel blow: the servant girl refused the poet in terms which admitted no dubiety. Burns wrote a philosophic reply, but at the same time he felt deeply, and therefore set out for Irvine in despondent mood. The enterprise so inauspiciously begun had a disastrous ending. His shop in Irvine caught fire, and he was reduced to absolute poverty. Finally he had to return. During the months which he spent at Irvine—from midsummer 1781 to March 1782—he brooded much over his sorrows. He wrote melancholy letters to his father, and seems at one time to have contemplated suicide. It is therefore not to be wondered at that such poetical compositions as have been preserved from this period strike a mournful note. "Winter, a Dirge," afterwards described by Burns as "the eldest of my printed pieces," is said to have been written then.

Back to the work of the farm, Burns was not long in throwing aside his love-sorrow. Although Murdoch had noticed at Alloway that Robert had a poor ear for music and a most untunable voice, yet at this time the disappointed lover practised assiduously the fiddle and the German flute and acquired a certain amount of musical skill. His old joviality returned. His social powers were greater than ever. His knowledge of life and of the world had increased from his sojourn in the seaport town, and although up till this period he had known not the joys of the wine-cup, he was now able to mix fearlessly in convivial company and to take off his glass with the best of them. So he himself asserted; but there is strong evidence that with the licence of a poet he exaggerated his prowess as a drinker. He afterwards sang the joys of drinking with an alluring charm, and the Bacchanalian taint is thus early manifested in "John Barleycorn," an improvement on an old ballad. Entering with zest into all forms of rustic gaiety, he attended balls and paid more or less court to every country maiden that took his passing fancy. None of these attachments were of a lasting nature, but nevertheless they inspired several of his love-songs, "Mary Morison," "The Rigs of Barley," "My Nannie, Oh," and others.

MARY MORISON

O Mary, at thy window be!
  It is the wished, the trysted hour!
Those smiles and glances let me see,
  That makes the miser's treasure poor:
How blithely wad I bide the stoure,
  A weary slave frae sun to sun,
Could I the rich reward secure—
  The lovely Mary Morison!

Yestreen, when to the trembling string,
 The dance gaed through the lighted ha',
To thee my fancy took its wing—
 I sat, but neither heard nor saw.
Though this was fair, and that was braw,
 And yon the toast of a' the town,
I sighed, and said amang them a',
 "Ye are na Mary Morison!"

O Mary, canst thou wreck his peace
 Wha for thy sake wad gladly die?
Or canst thou break that heart of his
 Whase only faut is loving thee?
If love for love thou wilt na gi'e,
 At least be pity to me shown;
A thought ungentle canna be
 The thought o' Mary Morison.

Thus early Burns showed his preference for the lyric. The song "Mary Morison" is a masterpiece: nothing in it can be wished otherwise: it has the unerring touch of the trained craftsman. Burns seems all at once to have cast his shackles from him and to have bounded forward, taking a short cut to perfection. Doubtless, like most young poets, he had experimented with various poetic forms, but of such "juvenilia" singularly little remains. Moreover, much of his apprenticeship work was never committed to writing, for he had an extraordinary gift of composing a whole poem in his head, of correcting and polishing it without reference to paper, and, if he were satisfied with it, of then writing it out from memory. This characteristic must be borne in mind, for it explains how he was afterwards able to produce a large body of poetry without apparent effort, and how on that account he came to be regarded as a marvellously inspired poet, untaught by rules of art. Curiously enough, all his earliest models were English. He had really few opportunities of making himself acquainted with the masterpieces of old Scottish poetry. Indeed, probably all the Scottish verse he knew had been in the form of songs and ballads learnt orally. His ambition had been towards the speaking and writing of correct English. But in 1782 he discovered Fergusson's poems, and thereafter he never faltered in his allegiance to the Scotch vernacular as a medium of literary expression. As was his habit, he selected a particular poem for study and imitation, criticising it line by line and aspiring always to improve upon the model. Thus many of his poems are directly suggested by those of Fergusson, but in execution and technique he soon left his master far behind. Had he not been superabundantly gifted with imagination, this method of imitation might have proved exceedingly dangerous, for there was every chance of his becoming nothing but a cold copyist. It was from his study of Fergusson that he developed that inspired use of dialect which had been absent from Scottish poetry since the days of Allan Ramsay. But the first work in which he evinced this peculiar power over dialect was not due to Fergusson. "The Death and Dying Words of

Poor Mailie," a humorous poem with a serious lesson, was suggested by Skinner's "Ewie wi' the Crookit Horn," or by Hamilton's "Last Dying Words of Bonny Heck," and shows not only a complete mastery of dialect, but also a certain dramatic deftness in the telling of a story which serves to rivet the reader's attention. In this poem and in its companion piece, "Poor Mailie's Elegy," Burns discovered the great secret of how to select from the world of commonplaces some incident of daily life, of how to illuminate it with poetic imagination without any sacrifice of naturalness and truth, and of how to work upon the sympathies of the reader so that he seems to see with the eyes of the poet himself. None of Burns's poetry, certainly none of his earlier poetry, was ever written with deliberate intent to publish. Out of pure exaltation of spirit and unhampered by the cramping fear of criticism, he sang to please himself.

While Burns was thus unconsciously realising his poetic mission things were not going well with the household at Lochlea. The old bad luck pursued his father's affairs. William Burnes fell into arrears with his rent and became involved in a lawsuit about the conditions of his lease. He had grown old and feeble, and in June 1783 it became evident that the hand of death was upon him. He lingered on till February 13, 1784, when he died. His body was laid to rest in Alloway Kirkyard. His last hours were embittered by the fear of a debtors' prison, for the lawsuit had been decided against him and he had been adjudged bankrupt. The family was dispossessed of the farm, the stock and plenishing being sold off to satisfy the landlord's claim. The wages of Robert, Gilbert, and the other grown-up members of the family had not been paid, and it was only by ranking as creditors on their father's estate that they were able to save a few belongings from the general wreck. The two brothers, shortly before the crisis—at Martinmas, 1783, to be exact—had taken a farm sublet to them by a lawyer, Gavin Hamilton, afterwards the firm friend of the poet. It lay not far from the little town of Mauchline and was called Mossgiel. To this new farm the whole household removed after the death of William Burnes.

The two brothers entered upon their tenancy with high hopes and good resolutions. Robert spared no pains: "I read farming books—I calculated crops—I attended markets." But their slender capital left no margin for contingencies. They were supplied with bad seed. They lost half of their poor crop through a late harvest. Hopes being thus blasted, the good resolutions, at least on Robert's part, did not stand long against adversity. He gradually left the management of the farm to his younger brother, and though he did his share of the manual labour and toiled sorely, yet his heart was not in his task. The claims of poesy became insistent. After he had done his day's work he used to retire to a little garret, lit by a narrow roof-light, to transcribe the verses which he had composed in the fields. These were no longer confined to passionate love-lyrics, but touched, at all points, the life with which he was familiar. Variety is now the characteristic where before there had almost been monotony. During the two years from 1784 to 1786 he poured forth a continuous stream of poetry, extraordinary in volume and depth, but not altogether surprising when regard is had to the severe discipline and training to which he had previously subjected himself. At the first he wrote with no thought of publishing, and thus his earlier work is very intimately associated with his personality.

Especially is this the case with his Epistles. These letters to his familiar friends, generally written off-hand and with all the ease of a simple reply to a correspondent, are full of revelations of his real life, and thus constitute biography of a somewhat unconscious kind. One of his associates in the Bachelors' Club was the schoolmaster at Irvine, David Sillar, son of a Tarbolton farmer. Him Burns addressed in an epistle as "Davie, a Brother-Poet, Lover, Ploughman, and Fiddler." "The Epistle to Davie," after alluding to the joys and sorrows of the poet's daily life, in several stanzas of homely philosophy marked by a cheery optimism, rises almost to lyric fervour in the praise of love. In the last stanza, a sort of anti-climax, Burns, as if half-apologising for his work, shows rare modesty and much sly humour.

THE EPISTLE TO DAVIE

While winds frae aff Ben Lomond blaw,
And bar the doors wi' driving snaw,
And hing us owre the ingle,
I set me down to pass the time,
And spin a verse or twa o' rhyme,
In hamely westlin' jingle.
While frosty winds blaw in the drift,
Ben to the chimla lug,
I grudge a wee the great folk's gift,
That live sae bien an' snug :
I tent less, and want less,
Their roomy fireside ;
But hanker, and canker,
To see their cursèd pride.

It's hardly in a b dy's power
To keep, at times, frae being sour,
To see how things are shared ;
How best o' chiels are whiles in want,
While coofs on countless thousands rant,
And ken na how to ware't :
But, Davie, lad, ne'er fash your head,
Though we ha'e little gear,
We're fit to win our daily bread,
As lang's we're hale and fier :
"Mair spier na, no fear na,"
Auld age ne'er mind a feg,
The last o't, the warst o't,
Is only but to beg.

To lie in kilns and barns at e'en,
When banes are crazed, and bluid is thin,
Is, doubtless, great distress ;

Yet then content could make us blest ;
E'en then, sometimes we'd snatch a taste
Of truest happiness.
The honest heart that's free frae a'
Intended fraud or guile,
However fortune kick the ba',
Has aye some cause to smile,
And mind still, you'll find still,
A comfort this nae sma' ;
Nae mair then, we'll care then,
Nae farther can we fa'.

What though, like commoners of air,
We wander out, we know not where,
But either house or hall ?
Yet Nature's charms, the hills and woods,
The sweeping vales, and foaming floods,
Are free alike to all.
In days when daisies deck the ground,
And blackbirds whistle clear,
With honest joy our hearts will bound
To see the coming year :
On braes when we please, then,
We'll sit an' sowth a tune ;
Syne rhyme till't, we'll time till't,
And sing't when we hae done.

It's no in titles nor in rank ;
It's no in wealth like Lon'on bank,
To purchase peace and rest ;
It's no in making muckle, mair :
It's no in books ; it's no in lear,
To make us truly blest :
If happiness ha'e not her seat
And centre in the breast,

We may be wise, or rich, or great,
But never can be blest!
Nae treasures, nor pleasures,
Could make us happy lang:
The heart aye's the part aye,
That makes us right or wrang.

Think ye, that sic as you and I,
Wha drudge and drive through wet an' dry,
Wi' never-ceasing toil;
Think ye, are we less blest than they,
Wha scarcely tent us in their way,
As hardly worth their while?
Alas! how aft in haughty mood,
God's creatures they oppress!
Or else, neglecting a' that's guid,
They riot in excess!
Baith careless, and fearless
Of either heaven or hell;
Esteeming, and deeming
It a' an idle tale!

Then let us cheerfu' acquiesce;
Nor make our scanty pleasures less,
By pining at our state;
And, even should misfortunes come,
I, here wha sit, hae met wi' some,
An's thankfu' for them yet.
They gi'e the wit of age to youth;
They let us ken oursel';
They make us see the naked truth,
The real guid and ill.
Though losses, and crosses,
Be lessons right severe,
There's wit there, ye'll get there,
Ye'll find nae other where.

But tent me, Davie, ace o' hearts !
(To say aught less wad wrang the cartes,
And flattery I detest,)
This life has joys for you and I ;
And joys that riches ne'er could buy ;
And joys the very best.
There's a' the pleasures o' the heart,
The lover an' the frien' ;
Ye ha'e your Meg, your dearest part,
And I my darling Jean !
It wa ms me, it charms me,
To mention but her name ;
It heats me, it beets me,
And sets me a' on flame !

O all ye Powers who rule above !
O Thou, whose very self art love !
Thou know'st my words sincere !
The life-blood streaming through my heart,
Or my more dear immortal part,
Is not more fondly dear !
When heart-corroding care and grief
Deprive my soul of rest,
Her dear idea brings relief
And solace to my breast.
Thou Being, All-seeing,
Oh, hear my fervent prayer !
Still take her, and make her
Thy most peculiar care !

All hail, ye tender feelings dear !
The smile of love, the friendly tear,
The sympathetic glow ;
Long since, this world's thorny ways
Had numbered out my weary days,
Had it not been for you !

Fate still has blest me with a friend
In every care and ill;
And oft a more endearing band,
A tie more tender still.
It lightens, it brightens
The tenebrific scene,
To meet with, and greet with
My Davie or my Jean!

Oh, how that Name inspires my style!
The words come skelpin rank and file,
Amaist before I ken!
The ready measure rins as fine,
As Phœbus and the famous Nine
Were glowrin' owre my pen.
My spaviet Pegasus will limp,
Till ance he's fairly het;
And then he'll hilch, and stilt, and jimp,
And rin an unco fit;
But lest then, the beast then
Should rue this hasty ride,
I'll 'light now, and dight now
His sweaty, wizened hide.

The "darling Jean" alluded to in "The Epistle to Davie" was Jean Armour, the most famous of all Burns's heroines. She first met the poet at the ball with which the Mauchline races closed in the year 1784. She was then about eighteen or nineteen years of age, and the poet was at once attracted to her. The courtship did not run smoothly, for Jean's father, a master mason in Mauchline, cordially detested Burns; why is not quite clear. Probably at some convivial meeting he had felt the lash of the poet's tongue and remembered it against his daughter's lover. Jean suffered much for Burns. The courtship was clandestine; her lover could not provide her with a home; her father was suspicious and latterly turned his daughter out of doors. But this is anticipating. Suffice it to say now that the lovers met frequently, and that although Burns wrote no songs directly in her honour, at this period, he made reference to her in several poems and showed no sign of his previous fickleness.

It is a remarkable feature of these two wonderful years at Mossgiel that Burns seemed all at once to realise the poetic material which lay around him. Never at a loss for a subject, he chose from the large mass of the old and familiar, and gave written expression to what had been mentally noted by countless observers. The poem "Halloween" illustrates this admirably. This is the picturesque way in which Carlyle puts it: "Our Halloween had passed and repassed, in rude awe and laughter, since the era of the Druids; but no Theocritus till Burns discerned in it the materials of a Scottish idyll." "Halloween" is rather long to quote. Modelled after Fergusson's "Leith Races," it is a descriptive poem of the true pastoral class—that is, its scenes and characters are real, not imaginary and idealistic. The Ayrshire peasantry are sketched as they really appeared on an occasion of old-time merriment such as Halloween, that festival of pagan rites which celebrated the last night of the harvest season.

Burns exposes the credulity and superstition of the rustics with kindly strokes of humour, but in the midst of broad farce he intersperses delightful sketches of inanimate Nature without the slightest trace of incongruity. Thus he makes one of the characters, "wanton widow Leezie," steal from the house wherein sat the merry party and go out—braving witches and warlocks all the while—to a small stream, there to perform a charm, namely, "to dip her left sark-sleeve in." The stream is thus described:

> Whyles owre a linn the burnie plays,
> As thro' the glen it wimpl't;
> Whyles round a rocky scar it strays;
> Whyles in a wiel it dimpl't;
> Whyles glitter'd to the nightly rays,
> Wi' bickerin', dancin' dazzle;
> Whyles cookit underneath the braes,
> Below the spreading hazel,
> Unseen that night.

But Lizzie's nerves were all on edge, and in the very next stanza—the poet shall tell it:

> Amang the brachens on the brae,
> Between her an' the moon,
> The Deil, or else an outler quey,
> Gat up an' gae a croon:
> Poor Leezie's heart maist lap the hool;
> Near lav'rock height she jumpit,
> But mist a fit, an' in the pool
> Out-owre the lugs she plumpit,
> Wi' a plunge that night.

BURNS & HIS POETRY

In "Poor Mailie's Elegy" Burns had regarded the beasts of the field as having feelings akin to those of human beings and as having a certain claim upon man's humanity. He now gave more powerful expression to the universal brotherhood of man with Nature in a poem which, apart altogether from the sentiment, must be reckoned as a piece of consummate craftsmanship. One day, when ploughing, Burns turned up the nest of a field-mouse. The little animal went scurrying away in fright, and a serving-man, named Blane, seized a stick to kill it. Burns stopped him, saying: "He's done ye no harm." In the evening Burns composed the following poem and, after reading it to Blane, said, "What do ye think o' the mouse now?"

TO A MOUSE

ON TURNING HER UP IN HER NEST WITH THE PLOUGH, NOVEMBER 1785

Wee, sleekit, cow'rin', tim'rous beastie,
O what a panic's in thy breastie!
Thou need na start awa sae hasty,
Wi' bickering brattle!
I wad be laith to rin an' chase thee
Wi' murd'ring pattle!

I'm truly sorry man's dominion
Has broken Nature's social union,
An' justifies that ill opinion
Which makes thee startle
At me, thy poor earth-born companion,
An' fellow-mortal!

I doubt na, whiles, but thou may thieve ;
What then ? poor beastie, thou maun live !
A daimen icker in a thrave
'S a sma' request :
I'll get a blessin' wi' the lave,
And never miss't !

Thy wee bit housie, too, in ruin !
Its silly wa's the win's are strewin' :
And naething, now, to big a new ane,
O' foggage green !
An' bleak December's winds ensuin'
Baith snell an' keen !

Thou saw the fields laid bare an' waste
An' weary winter comin' fast,
An' cozie here, beneath the blast,
Thou thought to dwell,
Till, crash ! the cruel coulter past
Out thro' thy cell.

That wee bit heap o' leaves an' stibble
Has cost thee mony a weary nibble !
Now thou's turn'd out, for a' thy trouble,
But house or hald,
To thole the winter's sleety dribble
An' cranreuch cauld !

But, Mousie, thou art no thy lane
In proving foresight may be vain :
The best laid schemes o' mice an' men
Gang aft a-gley,
An' lea'e us nought but grief an' pain,
For promised joy.

Still thou art blest, compared wi' me !
The present only toucheth thee :

> But, Och ! I backward cast my e'e
> On prospects drear !
> An' forward, tho' I canna see,
> I guess an' fear !

A year later, in April 1786, Burns was turning over a field with the plough and the ploughshare cut through a mountain daisy. Burns at once immortalised it. Years afterwards Wordsworth made a pilgrimage to Mossgiel and bethought him of the "wee, modest, crimson-tippèd flower." He thus records his visit :

> "There," said the stripling, pointing with much pride
> Towards a low roof, with green trees half-concealed,
> "Is Mossgiel farm ; and that's the very field
> Where Burns plough'd up the Daisy." Far and wide
> A plain below stretched seaward, while, descried
> Above sea-clouds, the peaks of Arran rose ;
> And by that simple notice, the repose
> Of earth, sky, sea, and air was vivified.
> Beneath the random field of clod or stone,
> Myriads of daisies have shone forth in flower
> Near the lark's nest, and in their natural hour
> Have passed away : less happy than the one
> That, by the unwilling ploughshare, died to prove
> The tender charm of poetry and love.

But it is doubtful if the poem about the daisy really equals "To a Mouse" in natural simplicity. The moralising bias of the age is found in both poems: but it is more evident in the later "To a Daisy," where the lesson is conveyed in five stanzas of pure English in a style reminiscent of Gray.

BURNS & HIS POETRY

TO A MOUNTAIN DAISY

ON TURNING ONE DOWN WITH THE PLOUGH IN APRIL 1786

Wee, modest, crimson-tippèd flower,
Thou's met me in an evil hour ;
For I maun crush amang the stoure
Thy slender stem ;
To spare thee now is past my power,
Thou bonnie gem.

Alas ! it's no thy neebor sweet,
The bonnie lark, companion meet,
Bending thee 'mang the dewy weet,
Wi' sprecklèd breast !
When upward-springing, blithe, to greet
The purpling east.

Cauld blew the bitter biting north
Upon thy early, humble birth ;
Yet cheerfully thou glinted forth
Amid the storm,
Scarce reared above the parent earth
Thy tender form.

The flaunting flowers our gardens yield,
High shelt'ring woods and wa's maun shield ;
But thou beneath the random bield
O' clod or stane,
Adorns the histie stibble-field,
Unseen, alane.

There, in thy scanty mantle clad,
Thy snawy bosom sunward spread,
Thou lifts thy unassuming head
In humble guise ;
But now the share uptears thy bed,
And low thou lies !

Such is the fate of artless maid,
Sweet flow'ret of the rural shade!
By love's simplicity betrayed,
And guileless trust,
Till she, like thee, all soiled, is laid
Low i' the dust.

Such is the fate of simple Bard,
On Life's rough ocean luckless starred!
Unskilful he to note the card
Of prudent lore,
Till billows rage, and gales blow hard,
And whelm him o'er!

Such fate to suffering Worth is given,
Who long with wants and woes has striven,
By human pride or cunning driven
To mis'ry's brink,
Till wrenched of every stay but Heaven,
He, ruined, sink!

Ev'n thou who mourn'st the Daisy's fate,
That fate is thine—no distant date;
Stern Ruin's ploughshare drives, elate,
Full on thy bloom,
Till crushed beneath the furrow's weight,
Shall be thy doom!

The same broad humanity and kindliness is seen in "The Auld Farmer's New-Year Morning Salutation to his Auld Mare Maggie." This poem smacks of the soil and shows clearly how Burns's genius was moulded and coloured by the agricultural life which he led. If it is true that, as Shakespeare avers, the hand of little employment hath the daintier sense, then an exception must be made in the case of the Ayrshire poet. No amount of toil, no amount of familiarity with the grosser aspects of life, hardened or made callous this peasant's heart. "In this homely but most kindly humorous poem," says Professor Shairp, "you have the whole toiling life of a ploughman and his horse, done off in two or three touches; and the elements of what may seem a commonplace, but was to Burns a most vivid experience, are made to live for ever. For a piece of good graphic Scotch, see how he describes the sturdy old mare in the plough setting her face to the furzy braes." Here is the passage:

Thou was a noble fittie-lan',
As e'er in tug or tow was drawn!
Aft thee an' I, in aught hours gaun,
In guid March-weather,
Hae turn'd sax rood beside our han',
For days thegither.

Thou never braing't, an' fetch't, an' fliskit,
But thy auld tail thou wad hae whiskit,
An' spread abreed thy weel-fill'd briskit,
Wi' pith an' pow'r,
Till sprittie knowes wad rair't and riskit,
An' slypet owre.

And now it is time for the poet by the magic of his art to cast a halo over the homes of the people he loved. Amongst the peasantry of Scotland it was then the habit to hold family worship every night. After the death of his father the poet became head of the family at Mossgiel and performed, with high seriousness, the duty of conducting the cottage worship. Nothing delighted him more than to hear a decent pious man, the head of a household, introducing family worship with the solemn words, "Let us worship God." This phrase was as a spark to the tinder of his imagination, and forms the text of his grand—though disguised—homily, "The Cotter's Saturday Night."

THE COTTER'S SATURDAY NIGHT

November chill blaws loud wi' angry sugh ;
The shortening winter-day is near a close ;
The miry beasts retreating frae the pleugh ;
The blackening trains o' craws to their repose :
The toil-worn Cotter frae his labour goes,
This night his weekly moil is at an end,
Collects his spades, his mattocks, and his hoes,
Hoping the morn in ease and rest to spend,
And weary, o'er the moor, his course does hameward bend.

At length his lonely cot appears in view,
Beneath the shelter of an agèd tree ;
The expectant wee-things, toddlin', stacher through
To meet their Dad, wi' flichterin' noise an' glee.
His wee bit ingle, blinking bonnily,
His clean hearthstane, his thriftie wifie's smile,
The lisping infant prattling on his knee,
Does a' his weary carking cares beguile,
And makes him quite forget his labour and his toil.

Belyve the elder bairns come drapping in,
At service out, amang the farmers roun',
Some ca' the pleugh, some herd, some tentie rin
A cannie errand to a neebor town :
Their eldest hope, their Jenny, woman grown,
In youthfu' bloom, love sparkling in her e'e,
Comes hame, perhaps, to shew a braw new gown,
Or deposite her sair-won penny-fee,
To help her parents dear, if they in hardship be.

Wi' joy unfeigned brothers and sisters meet,
An' each for other's weelfare kindly spiers :
The social hours, swift-winged, unnoticed fleet ;
Each tells the uncos that he sees or hears :
The parents, partial, eye their hopeful years ;
Anticipation forward points the view.
The mother, wi' her needle an' her shears,
Gars auld claes look amaist as weel's the new ;
The father mixes a' wi' admonition due.

Their master's an' their mistress's command,
The younkers a' are warnèd to obey ;
An' mind their labours wi' an eydent hand,
An' ne'er, though out o' sight, to jauk or play :
" An' O ! be sure to fear the Lord alway !
An' mind your duty duly, morn an' night !
Lest in temptation's path ye gang astray,
Implore His counsel and assisting might :
They never sought in vain that sought the Lord
aright ! "

But hark ! a rap comes gently to the door ;
Jenny, wha kens the meaning o' the same,
Tells how a neebor lad cam' o'er the moor,
To do some errands, and convoy her hame.

The wily mother sees the conscious flame
Sparkle in Jenny's e'e, and flush her cheek ;
With heart-struck anxious care, inquires his name,
While Jenny hafflins is afraid to speak :
Weel pleased the mother hears it's nae wild, worthless rake.

Wi' kindly welcome Jenny brings him ben,
A strappan youth ; he takes the mother's eye ;
Blithe Jenny sees the visit's no ill ta'en ;
The father cracks of horses, pleughs, and kye :
The youngster's artless heart o'erflows wi' joy.
But blate and laithfu', scarce can weel behave ;
The mother, wi' a woman's wiles, can spy
What makes the youth sae bashfu' an' sae grave ;
Weel pleased to think her bairn's respected like the lave.

O happy love ! where love like this is found !
O heartfelt raptures ! bliss beyond compare !
I've pacèd much this weary, mortal round,
And sage experience bids me this declare—
" If Heaven a draught of heavenly pleasure spare,
One cordial in this melancholy vale,
'Tis when a youthful, loving, modest pair,
In other's arms, breathe out the tender tale,
Beneath the milk-white thorn that scents the evening gale."

Is there, in human form, that bears a heart—
A wretch ! a villain ! lost to love and truth !
That can, with studied, sly, ensnaring art,
Betray sweet Jenny's unsuspecting youth ?
Curse on his perjured arts ! dissembling, smooth !
Are honour, virtue, conscience, all exiled ?
Is there no pity, no relenting ruth,

Points to the parents fondling o'er their child?
Then paints the ruined maid, and their distraction wild?

But now the supper crowns their simple board,
The halesome parritch, chief o' Scotia's food:
The soupe their only Hawkie does afford,
That 'yont the hallan snugly chows her cood:
The dame brings forth in complimental mood,
To grace the lad, her weel-hained kebbuck, fell;
An' aft he's prest, an' aft he ca's it guid;
The frugal wifie, garrulous, will tell,
How 'twas a towmond auld, sin' lint was i' the bell.

The cheerfu' supper done, wi' serious face,
They, round the ingle, form a circle wide;
The sire turns o'er, wi' patriarchal grace,
The big ha' Bible, ance his father's pride:
His bonnet rev'rently is laid aside,
His lyart haffets wearing thin an' bare;
Those strains that once did sweet in Zion glide,
He wales a portion with judicious care;
And "Let us worship God!" he says, with solemn air.

They chant their artless notes in simple guise;
They tune their hearts, by far the noblest aim:
Perhaps "Dundee's" wild warbling measures rise,
Or plaintive "Martyrs," worthy of the name:
Or noble "Elgin" beets the heavenward flame,
The sweetest far of Scotia's holy lays:
Compared with these, Italian trills are tame;
The tickled ears no heartfelt raptures raise;
Nae unison hae they, with our Creator's praise.

The priest-like father reads the sacred page,
How Abram was the friend of God on high;
Or, Moses bade eternal warfare wage
With Amalek's ungracious progeny;

Or how the royal bard did groaning lie
Beneath the stroke of Heaven's avenging ire;
Or, Job's pathetic plaint, and wailing cry;
Or rapt Isaiah's wild, seraphic fire;
Or other holy Seers that tune the sacred lyre.

Perhaps the Christian volume is the theme,
How guiltless blood for guilty man was shed;
How He, who bore in Heaven the second name,
Had not on earth whereon to lay His head:
How His first followers and servants sped;
The precepts sage they wrote to many a land:
How he, who lone in Patmos banishèd,
Saw in the sun a mighty angel stand;
And heard great Bab'lon's doom pronounced by
Heaven's command.

Then kneeling down, to Heaven's Eternal King,
The saint, the father, and the husband prays:
Hope "springs exulting on triumphant wing,"
That thus they all shall meet in future days:
There, ever bask in uncreated rays,
No more to sigh, or shed the bitter tear,
Together hymning their Creator's praise,
In such society, yet still more dear;
While circling Time moves round in an eternal sphere.

Compared with this, how poor Religion's pride,
In all the pomp of method, and of art,
When men display to congregations wide,
Devotion's every grace, except the heart!
The Power, incensed, the pageant will desert,
The pompous strain, the sacerdotal stole;
But haply, in some cottage far apart,
May hear, well pleased, the language of the soul;
And in His Book of Life the inmates poor enrol.

Then homeward all take off their several way ;
The youngling cottagers retire to rest :
The parent pair their secret homage pay,
And proffer up to Heaven the warm request
That He who stills the raven's clamorous nest,
And decks the lily fair in flowery pride,
Would, in the way His wisdom sees the best,
For them and for their little ones provide ;
But chiefly, in their hearts with grace divine preside.

From scenes like these, old Scotia's grandeur springs,
That makes her loved at home, revered abroad :
Princes and lords are but the breath of kings,
" An honest man's the noblest work of God " :
And certes, in fair virtue's heavenly road,
The cottage leaves the palace far behind ;
What is a lordling's pomp ? a cumbrous load,
Disguising oft the wretch of human kind,
Studied in arts of Hell, in wickedness refined !

O Scotia ! my dear, my native soil !
For whom my warmest wish to Heaven is sent !
Long may thy hardy sons of rustic toil
Be blest with health, and peace, and sweet content !
And, O ! may Heaven their simple lives prevent
From Luxury's contagion, weak and vile !
Then, howe'er crowns and coronets be rent,
A virtuous populace may rise the while,
And stand a wall of fire around their much-loved Isle.

O Thou ! who poured the patriotic tide
That streamed through Wallace's undaunted heart
Who dared to nobly stem tyrannic pride,
Or nobly die, the second glorious part,
(The patriot's God, peculiarly Thou art,

His friend, inspirer, guardian, and reward !)
O never, never, Scotia's realm desert ;
But still the patriot, and the patriot bard,
In bright succession raise, her ornament and guard !

"The Cotter's Saturday Night" is the most popular of Burns's longer poems. It has been translated into twelve languages and has evoked widespread admiration. The topic is happily chosen and calculated to arouse universal sympathy. Deft touches of sly humour and of simple realism differentiate this poem from those of a frankly evangelical type. The portrait of William Burnes, the priest-like father—"his lyart haffets wearing thin an' bare"—gives it an autobiographic and personal interest. It is a touching sketch of pure family life. It is in itself ennobling. The parts that affect most are the faithful descriptions of what were then regarded as the most ordinary conventions. In this connection a good story is related. Mrs. Dunlop, the friend and correspondent of the poet, gave the poem to her housekeeper to read ; the servant in returning it paid the poetry a high tribute, all unconscious to herself : "Gentlemen and leddies may think muckle o' this ; but for me it's naething but what I saw i' my faither's hoose every day, an' I dinna see hoo he could hae tel't it ony ither way."

But in spite of all these charms the poem does not reach Burns's height of art. Its plan was taken from Fergusson's "Farmer's Ingle" ; but the stanza followed the manner of Shenstone, for Burns as yet was unacquainted with Spenser.

This difficult stanza was not one to which the poet had habituated himself. The poem is unequal: the first half written in Scotch and the second half written in English have each been claimed as superior to the other by different schools of critics. Burns did not rid himself entirely of the pastoral convention. The homes of the Scottish peasantry were not and are not idyllic. The realism of the first half of the poem is glossed over with that sentimentality so characteristic of the eighteenth century, and in the last stanzas the poet merges into an obtrusive didacticism. Such are the objections of the critics; but "Burns's genius," says Lockhart, "would suffer more in estimation by being contemplated in the absence of this poem than of any other single poem he has left us." Who would wish it otherwise?

When Burns wrote "The Cotter's Saturday Night" he undoubtedly sketched the scene from life. The simple fireside piety of the home delighted him, but none knew better than he that this was but one aspect of the religious life of the peasantry. In the Kirk of Scotland there was much sectarianism, and the public brawling contrasted strangely with the peaceful picture of family worship. As Crabbe provided the sordid picture to be placed alongside Goldsmith's "Deserted Village," so Burns in his satires provided several companion pieces to be read as corrective to "The Saturday Night." His greatest satires are levelled at that congeries of conflicting interests which in his time constituted the Church. Burns was early suspected of heretical principles. He lived in a time of great ecclesiastical unrest, both within and without the Church. He had read the polemics of religion, and in the churchyard debates which, with drinking at the inn, then formed the chief means of whiling away the time between sermons on a Sunday, he had been distinguished for his unorthodox views. Within the Church two opposing schools had arisen: one, termed the "Auld Lights," steadfastly resisted any alteration in the extreme doctrine of Calvinism; the other, termed the "New Lights," favoured a relaxation of the ecclesiastical bonds and the abolition of clerical subscription to the Confession of Faith. Both Auld Lights and New Lights were too dogmatic for Burns, but the narrow intolerance of Old-Lightism was more repellent:

> But I gae mad at their grimaces,
> Their sighin', cantin' grace-proud faces,
> Their three-mile prayers, an' hauf-mile graces,
> Their raxin conscience,
> Whase greed, revenge, an' pride disgraces
> Waur nor their nonsense.

An opportunity of satirising the Auld Lights soon occurred. Two champions of the strict school had fallen out about a question of parish boundaries, and when the case was being debated the two fiery divines abused each other in the open court, to the great amusement of the ungodly. Burns at once wrote "The Twa

Herds," by some considered his most powerful satire, in which he admonished with mock seriousness the two disputants. The poem had an extensive circulation in manuscript in Ayrshire, and at the time met with a roar of applause, but its interest for the general reader has perished with the quarrels which called it forth.

In " The Twa Herds " Burns really satirised a party : in " Holy Willie's Prayer " he scarified an elder associated with it. The Kirk possessed and exercised considerable disciplinary powers, and to resist the Kirk meant the incurring not only of the usual legal punishments, but of social boycott likewise. Mr. Gavin Hamilton, the landlord of Mossgiel, had been refused baptism for his child because he had gone on a journey on a certain Sunday in spite of the minister's warning, and, more heinous still, on another Sunday he had ordered some potatoes to be dug for the family dinner ! Hamilton fought the case in the Church courts and won it, chiefly through the eloquence of a lawyer friend, Robert Aiken of Ayr. One of the leaders in the persecution was an elder named William Fisher, and the petty malice shown by this man fired Burns to satirise him in " Holy Willie's Prayer." The poet pretends to overhear Holy Willie at his devotions calling down vengeance on all his enemies. The two stanzas immediately referring to Hamilton are the mildest parts of this scathing attack :

> Lord, mind Gaw'n Hamilton's deserts,
> He drinks an' swears, an' plays at cartes,

Yet has sae monie takin' arts,
Wi' grit an' sma',
Frae God's ain priest the people's hearts
He steals awa'.

An' whan we chasten'd him therefore,
Thou kens how he bred sic a splore
As set the world in a roar
O' laughin' at us ;
Curse thou his basket and his store,
Kail and potatoes.

These satires, although aimed at the strictly orthodox school, do not necessarily imply that Burns was a New Light. It is true that his friends belonged to the latter party, but there is evidence that while Burns was willing to break a spear on behalf of his friends, his real position was that of Mercutio—"a plague on both your houses." In one of his letters he maintained that a sectarian turn of mind had always a tendency to narrow and illiberalise the heart, and in a "Postscript" to "The Epistle to William Simson" he satirised both parties impartially. The epistle itself is interesting as showing that Burns was now deliberately setting himself to emulate his famous predecessors :

My senses wad be in a creel,
Should I but dare a hope to speel,
Wi' Allan, or wi' Gilbertfield,
The braes o' fame ;
Or Fergusson, the writer-chiel,
A deathless name.

* * * * *

Ramsay an' famous Fergusson
Gied Forth an' Tay a lift aboon :
Yarrow and Tweed, to mony a tune,
Owre Scotland rings
While Irwin, Lugar, Ayr, an' Doon
Naebody sings.

* * * * *

We'll sing auld Coila's plains an' fells,
Her moors red-brown wi' heather bells,
Her banks an' braes, her dens an' dells,
Where glorious Wallace
Aft bure the gree, as story tells,
Frae Southron billies.

At Wallace' name, what Scottish blood
But boils up in a spring-tide flood?
Oft have our fearless fathers strode
By Wallace' side,
Still pressing onward, red-wat-shod,
Or glorious dy'd!

In 1785 Burns addressed a general satire to the "unco guid," either New or Old, to whichever denomination they may have belonged. The more general the satire the less venomous it is bound to be ; but as this satire depends, for its force, less than others upon the exigencies of the moment, it is here printed in full. The second last stanza is often quoted :

TO THE UNCO GUID

O, ye wha are sae guid yoursel',
Sae pious and sae holy,
Ye've nought to do but mark and tell
Your neebours' faults and folly ;

Whase life is like a weel-gaun mill,
  Supplied wi' store o' water,
The heapet happer's ebbing still,
  And still the clap plays clatter.

Hear me, ye venerable core,
  As counsel for poor mortals,
That frequent pass douce Wisdom's door
  For glaikit Folly's portals ;
I, for their thoughtless, careless sakes
  Would here propone defences,
Their donsie tricks, their black mistakes,
  Their failings and mischances.

Ye see your state wi' theirs compared,
  And shudder at the niffer,
But cast a moment's fair regard,
  What mak's the mighty differ ?
Discount what scant occasion gave
  That purity ye pride in,
And (what's aft mair than a' the lave)
  Your better art o' hiding.

Think, when your castigated pulse
  Gi'es now and then a wallop,
What ragings must his veins convulse,
  That still eternal gallop !
Wi' wind and tide fair i' your tail,
  Right on ye scud your sea-way ;
But in the teeth o' baith to sail,
  It mak's an unco leeway.

See Social Life and Glee sit down,
  All joyous and unthinking,
Till, quite transmugrified, they're grown
  Debauchery and Drinking :

O, would they stay to calculate
Th' eternal consequences ;
Or—your more dreaded hell to state,—
Damnation of expenses !

Ye high, exalted, virtuous dames,
Tied up in godly laces,
Before ye gi'e poor Frailty names,
Suppose a change o' cases ;
A dear-loved lad, convenience snug,
A treacherous inclination—
But, let me whisper i' your lug,
Ye're aiblins nae temptation.

Then gently scan your brother man,
Still gentler sister woman ;
Though they may gang a kennin wrang,
To step aside is human :
One point must still be greatly dark,
The moving why they do it ;
And just as lamely can ye mark
How far, perhaps, they rue it.

Who made the heart, 'tis He alone
Decidedly can try us,
He knows each chord—its various tone,
Each spring—its various bias :
Then at the balance let's be mute,
We never can adjust it ;
What's done we partly may compute,
But know not what's resisted.

The greatest of all Burns's satires on religion is "The Holy Fair." At the time of "the Sacrament" it was the custom for all the people of the parish to assemble at or near the kirk to hold a "preaching," or open-air conventicle. Several clergymen assisted at these services, and temporary platforms were often erected in the Kirkyard. These ceremonies might last a week, and the people brought provisions with them and often camped out in the fields. The preachings were generally arranged at different times for neighbouring parishes, so that there was often an influx of strangers. Such solemn scenes in course of time became occasions of drunken rout and revelry, and degenerated into a perfect carnival of licence. Drunk with enthusiasm, drunk with "nappy," fanatically drunk, rival factions debated, argued, wrangled, and even came to blows. Others, more ungodly, went to pray but remained to jest, and with drink and song and merry dance gave little heed to the morrow. It is now difficult to conceive of such a travesty of religion : the pencil of a Hogarth or a Wilkie could scarcely portray the scene. But with the eye of an artist Burns saw what was capable of being reproduced, and, with implacable, indignant scorn, painted in faithful colours the disgraceful orgies of the holy fair. It was a sharp lesson to clergy and to people alike, and it did much to purify religious life.

It is impossible to mention in this little book even a tithe of the poems which Burns threw off with seeming careless ease in the two years (1784–1786) now under review. The caustic wit of the great social satire "The Twa Dogs," the naive drollery of the personal satire "Death and Dr. Hornbook," the playful wisdom of the admirable "To a Louse," the vivid description in the reckless "Scotch Drink," the grand prophetic utterance in "The Vision," the austere pessimism of "Man was made to mourn," the joy of life in "The Jolly Beggars," can only be realised by a perusal of the poems themselves.

"The Jolly Beggars" is a musical drama of which Burns thought so little that he never published it, and indeed he seems to have forgotten about it altogether. It was published after the death of the poet. Nevertheless it disputes with "The Holy Fair" and "Tam o' Shanter" the honour of being Burns's greatest work. The inception of the poem was similar to that of nearly all his other productions. Happening to be passing an alehouse of the lowest class, kept by one Poosie Nansie, he heard the noise of revelry. Accompanied by a friend, he entered and found an assembly of vagrants, each contributing something characteristic to the performance. Such a scene filled Burns with delight, and a few days afterwards he wrote "The Jolly Beggars," with songs for each of the characters he had seen. Matthew Arnold says: "'The Jolly Beggars' has a breadth, truth, and power which make the famous scene in Auerbach's cellar, of Goethe's 'Faust,' seem artificial and tame beside it, and which are only matched by Shakespeare and Aristophanes."

During all this great period of productivity

the worldly affairs of Burns had been going ill. Mossgiel was a failure and the poet had no prospects. Jean Armour's father, alarmed at the influence which Burns possessed with his daughter, had her removed to Paisley, but not before Burns and she had been privately married according to the civil, but not the ecclesiastical, law. Old Armour, on this fact coming to his ears, flew into a rage and mutilated the document in which Burns had acknowledged Jean as his wife, and thus destroyed the legal evidence. Burns made many humble advances, and even offered to work as a common labourer for Jean's support, but all in vain. The Mauchline mason on no account would have the future national poet as his son-in-law. He actually set the law in motion against him, and Burns, afraid of imprisonment, left Mossgiel for a time and went into hiding. He secured a situation as a book-keeper on a plantation in Jamaica and prepared to leave Scotland, but lack of funds caused some months' delay. Some of his friends suggested the publication of his poems in order to raise his passage-money. Overtures were therefore made, and a printer in Kilmarnock, one John Wilson, was found willing to undertake the printing if the price of the paper was guaranteed. But alas ! even for this the poet was unable to provide the few necessary pounds. Ultimately Gavin Hamilton suggested that a sufficient number of subscribers might be found amongst the poet's friends to make failure impossible and profit not too remotely problematical. Many of the Ayrshire gentry rose to the occasion, particularly the small landed proprietors, men who were not far removed from the poet in social station and with whom he could meet on equal ground. A sufficient guarantee was soon obtained, and so it came that during June and July the poems constituting the first, or Kilmarnock, edition were passing through the press. With the exception of the most outrageous of the satires, most of the poems already mentioned were now printed, and in addition Burns wrote several pieces expressly for the volume.

Meanwhile Jean had returned from Paisley, and the poet, swallowing his pride, ventured to call at her house again. He was turned from the door, and in high dudgeon vowed never again to approach the Armours. He determined to look out for another wife. With great dispatch he selected one Mary Campbell, a nursemaid in the service of his friend Gavin Hamilton, and the pair agreed to marry. The whole circumstances of this love affair are obscure. Cromek, one of the earliest biographers of the poet, describes in great detail how the lovers stood by the side of a stream, laved their hands in the water, and, holding a Bible between them, promised to be faithful for ever. Mary presented him with a small plain Bible, while he on his part gave her one, in two volumes. These latter are now in the museum at Alloway. The date of this meeting is given, on the poet's own authority, as the second Sunday in May 1786. Mary set out for her home in Greenock to arrange matters among her friends for the approaching ceremony. Burns never saw her again. She died in October 1786. The poet wrote several poems to her: "Will ye go to the Indies, my Mary," "Prayer for Mary," "My Highland Lassie, O"; and some years later the memory of his lost love came to him, and inspired him to write a wonderful lyric in her honour. The episode of Highland Mary is one of the most romantic and strange in the chequered career of Burns.

All this time the poet was in an unhappy frame of mind. He seemed to rush from one misfortune to the other. His mental state may be judged from the numerous sad pieces which he now composed, particularly his "Farewell to the Banks of Ayr" and his "Bard's Epitaph."

FAREWELL TO THE BANKS OF AYR

The gloomy night is gath'ring fast,
Loud roars the wild inconstant blast,
Yon murky cloud is filled with rain,
I see it driving o'er the plain;
The hunter now has left the moor,
The scattered coveys meet secure,
While here I wander, prest with care,
Along the lonely banks of Ayr.

The Autumn mourns her rip'ning corn
By early winter's ravage torn;
Across her placid, azure sky,
She sees the scowling tempest fly:

Chill runs my blood to hear it rave;
I think upon the stormy wave,
Where many a danger I must dare,
Far from the bonnie banks of Ayr.

'Tis not the surging billows' roar,
'Tis not that fatal, deadly shore;
Tho' death in ev'ry shape appear,
The wretched have nc more to fear:
But round my heart the ties are bound,
That heart transpierc'd with many a wound:
These bleed afresh, those ties I tear,
To leave the bonnie banks of Ayr.

Farewell, old Coila's hills and dales,
Her heathy moors and winding vales;
The scenes where wretched fancy roves,
Pursuing past, unhappy loves!
Farewell my friends! Farewell my foes!
My peace with these, my love with those—
The bursting tears my heart declare,
Farewell, my bonnie banks of Ayr.

A BARD'S EPITAPH

Is there a whim-inspirèd fool,
Owre fast for thought, owre hot for rule,
Owre blate to seek, owre proud to snool?
Let him draw near;
And owre this grassy heap sing dool,
And drap a tear.

Is there a Bard of rustic song
Who, noteless, steals the crowds among,
That weekly this area throng?
O, pass not by!
But, with a frater-feeling strong,
Here, heave a sigh.

Is there a man, whose judgment clear
Can others teach the course to steer,
Yet runs, himself, life's mad career
          Wild as the wave ?
Here pause—and, through the starting tear,
          Survey this grave.

The poor inhabitant below
Was quick to learn, and wise to know,
And keenly felt the friendly glow
          And softer flame ;
But thoughtless follies laid him low,
          And stained his name !

Reader, attend ! Whether thy soul
Soars Fancy's flights beyond the pole,
Or darkling grubs this earthly hole
          In low pursuit ;
Know, prudent, cautious self-control
          Is wisdom's root.

The bard is, of course, Burns himself ; and, as Wordsworth has pointed out, the epitaph "is a sincere and solemn avowal ; a public declaration from his own will ; a confession at once devout, poetical, human ; a history in the shape of a prophecy." The cry for sympathy has not remained unanswered, and great as were the faults of Burns there is no poet who has had such eloquent defenders. It was always easy for Burns to teach others how to steer the course : he was an excellent counsellor, and the pity of it is that he too often "recked not his own rede." This is well illustrated in the "Epistle to a Young Friend," written in compliment to Mr. Aiken, the writer who had defended Gavin Hamilton against Holy Willie's crew. Andrew Hunter Aiken, the lawyer's eldest son, was then about to go to business, and Burns wrote him the following sound advice. The poem, composed in May 1786, was included in the Kilmarnock edition.

EPISTLE TO A YOUNG FRIEND

I lang ha'e thought, my youthfu' friend,
  A something to have sent you,
Though it should serve nae other end
  Than just a kind memento ;
But how the subject theme may gang,
  Let time and chance determine ;
Perhaps it may turn out a sang,
  Perhaps, turn out a sermon.

Ye'll try the world soon, my lad,
  And, Andrew dear, believe me,
Ye'll find mankind an unco squad,
  And muckle they may grieve ye :
For care and trouble set your thought,
  E'en when your end's attained ;
And a' your views may come to nought,
  Where every nerve is strained.

I'll no say men are villains a' ;
  The real, hardened wicked,
Wha ha'e nae check but human law,
  Are to a few restricted :
But och, mankind are unco weak,
  An' little to be trusted ;
If Self the wavering balance shake,
  It's rarely right adjusted !

Yet they wha fa' in fortune's strife,
  Their fate we shou'd na censure,
For still th' importan' end of life
  They equally may answer ;
A man may ha'e an honest heart,
  Though poortith hourly stare him ;
A man may tak' a neebor's part,
  Yet ha'e nae cash to spare him.

Aye free, aff han' your story tell,
  When wi' a bosom crony ;
But still keep something to yoursel'
  Ye scarcely tell to ony.
Conceal yoursel' as weel's ye can
  Fra critical dissection ;
But keek through every other man,
  Wi' sharpened, sly inspection.

The sacred lowe o' weel-placed love,
  Luxuriantly indulge it ;
But never tempt th' illicit rove,
  Though naething should divulge it :
I waive the quantum o' the sin,
  The hazard of concealing :
But och ! it hardens a' within,
  And petrifies the feeling !

To catch dame Fortune's golden smile,
  Assiduous wait upon her ;
And gather gear by every wile
  That's justified by honour ;
Not for to hide it in a hedge,
  Nor for a train attendant ;
But for the glorious privilege
  Of being independent.

The fear o' Hell's a hangman's whip
To haud the wretch in order ;
But where ye feel your honour grip,
Let that aye be your border ;
Its slightest touches, instant pause—
Debar a' side pretences ;
And resolutely keep its laws,
Uncaring consequences.

The Great Creator to revere,
Must sure become the creature ;
But still the preaching cant forbear,
And e'en the rigid feature :
Yet ne'er with wits profane to range,
Be complaisance extended ;
An atheist's laugh's a poor exchange
For Deity offended !

When ranting round in Pleasure's ring,
Religion may be blinded ;
Or if she gi'e a random sting,
It may be little minded ;
But when on Life we're tempest-driven,
A conscience but a canker—
A correspondence fixed wi' Heaven
Is sure a noble anchor !

Adieu, dear amiable youth !
Your heart can ne'er be wanting :
May Prudence, Fortitude, and Truth,
Erect your brow undaunting !
In ploughman phrase, " God send you speed,"
Still daily to grow wiser !
And may you better reck the rede,
Than ever did th' adviser !

On July 31, 1786, the poems left the press. The whole edition of 612 copies was sold out immediately, and so great was the demand that no copy could be spared for Mossgiel. The price of the copy was 3s.; it is now nearly £1200. The profit realised was some £20, and the first thing the poet did was to book his passage for Jamaica. But the ship was accidentally delayed at Greenock, and the fame of the poems having gone beyond Ayrshire, the friends of the poet did their best to keep him in Scotland, some suggesting one plan for his advancement, some another. Going abroad was a disagreeable necessity. Never hearty in the project, he was quite unable to decide what should be done. At last a criticism by Dr. Blacklock, the blind poet, who advised him to issue a second edition of the poems in Edinburgh, and assured him that they were likely to obtain "a more universal circulation than anything that has been printed within my memory," decided Burns to try his fortune in the capital. An article by Sibbald in "The Edinburgh Magazine" also encouraged him greatly. The upshot was that the ship sailed from Greenock without Burns.

In the autumn of 1786, either while the poems were passing through the press or immediately after, the poet produced the famous "The Twa Brigs," a dialogue modelled on Fergusson's "Dialogue between the Plainstanes and the Causeway," but immeasurably superior to it:

> Auld Brig appear'd of ancient Pictish race,
> The vera wrinkles Gothic in his face :
> New Brig was buskit in a braw new coat,
> That he at Lon'on frae ane Adams got.

Burns's poem is really a plea against that species of vandalism which on the ground of utility seeks to destroy what is old and artistic. The Auld Brig still stands in Ayr, but its rival, the New Brig, was swept away, as the poet prophesied :

> A Lesson sadly teaching to your cost,
> That Architecture's noble art is lost.

The famous song " The Lass o' Ballochmyle " is generally attributed to this period also, it having been sent to the heroine on November 18, 1786 ; but the poet definitely states that he wrote it in the spring :

I had roved out, as chance directed, in the favourite haunts of my muse, on the banks of the Ayr, to view Nature in all the gayety of the vernal year. The evening sun was flaming over the distant western hills ; not a breath stirred the crimson opening blossom, or the verdant spreading leaf. It was a golden moment for a poetic heart. I listened to the feathered warblers, pouring their harmony on every hand, with a congenial, kindred regard, and frequently turned out of my path lest I should disturb their little songs, or frighten them to another station. " Surely," said I to myself, " he must be a wretch indeed who, regardless of your harmonious endeavour to please him, can eye your elusive flights to discover your secret recesses, and to rob you of all the property Nature gives you—your dearest comforts, your hapless nestlings. Even the hoary hawthorn twig that shot across the way, what heart at such a time but must have been interested in its welfare, and wished it preserved from the rudely browsing cattle, or the withering eastern blast ? " Such was the scene, and such the hour, when in a corner of my prospect I spied one of the fairest pieces of Nature's workmanship that ever crowned a poetic landscape or met a poet's eye. What an hour of inspiration for a poet ! It would have raised plain, dull, historic prose into metaphor and measure. The enclosed song was the work of my return home, and perhaps it but poorly answers what might have been expected from such a scene.

Miss Wilhelmina Alexander, the daughter of the owner of Ballochmyle, to whom the poem and the letter were addressed, took no notice of either. Burns was offended, and when Mrs. Dunlop tried to excuse her, he said : " Had a half-witling lord written the poem, madam, would she have left it unanswered ? " Nevertheless the lady preserved both the letter and the poem, and in her old age was proud of the honour Burns had done her :

THE LASS O' BALLOCHMYLE

'Twas even—the dewy fields were green ;
On every blade the pearls hang ;
The zephyrs wantoned round the bean,
And bore its fragrant sweets alang ;

In every glen the mavis sang,
All Nature listening seemed the while,
Except where greenwood echoes rang,
Amang the braes o' Ballochmyle.

With careless step I onward strayed,
My heart rejoiced in Nature's joy,
When, musing in a lonely glade,
A maiden fair I chanced to spy :
Her look was like the Morning's eye,
Her air like Nature's vernal smile,
Perfection whispered, passing by,
Behold the lass o' Ballochmyle !

Fair is the morn in flowery May,
And sweet is night in autumn mild ;
When roving through the garden gay,
Or wandering in the lonely wild :
But Woman, Nature's darling child !
There all her charms she does compile ;
Ev'n there her other works are foiled
By the bonnie lass o' Ballochmyle.

O ! had she been a country maid,
And I the happy country swain,
Though sheltered in the lowest shed
That ever rose on Scotland's plain ;
Through weary winter's wind and rain,
With joy, with rapture I would toil ;
And nightly to my bosom strain
The bonnie lass o' Ballochmyle !

Then Pride might climb the slippery steep,
Where fame and honours lofty shine ;
And thirst of gold might tempt the deep,
Or downward seek the Indian mine ;

Give me the cot below the pine,
  To tend the flocks, or till the soil,
And every day have joys divine
  With the bonnie lass o' Ballochmyle.

The publication of the poems brought Burns many friends, the chief of whom were Professor Dugald Stewart, of Edinburgh, and Mrs. Dunlop, of Dunlop. Dugald Stewart had a country-house at Catrine, not far from Mossgiel, and one day he invited the young ploughman to dinner. At the table he met Lord Daer, a splendid young fellow whom he instantly liked. He who in "The Cotter's Saturday Night" had sneered at the lordling's pomp now began to make exceptions :

LINES ON MEETING WITH LORD DAER

This wot ye all whom it concerns,
I, Rhymer Rabin, alias Burns,
        October twenty-third,
A ne'er to be forgotten day,
Sae far I sprachled up the brae,
        I dinner'd wi' a Lord.

I've been at drunken writers' feasts,
Nay, been bitch-fou 'mang godly priests,
        Wi' rev'rence be it spoken ;
I've even join'd the honour'd jorum,
When mighty Squireships of the quorum
        Their hydra drouth did sloken.

But wi' a Lord—stand out my shin !
A Lord—a Peer—an Earl's son !
        Up higher yet, my bonnet !

An' sic a Lord—lang Scotch ells twa,
Our Peerage he o'erlooks them a'
As I look o'er my sonnet.

But, O for Hogarth's magic pow'r!
To show Sir Bardie's willyart glow'r,
And how he stared and stammer'd,
When goavan, as if led wi' branks
An' stumpin' on his ploughman shanks,
He in the parlour hammer'd.

I sidling sheltered in a nook,
An' at his Lordship steal't a look,
Like some portentous omen;
Except good sense and social glee,
An' (what surprised me) modesty,
I marked nought uncommon.

I watch'd the symptoms o' the Great,
The gentle pride, the lordly state,
The arrogant assuming;
The fient a pride, nae pride had he,
Nor sauce, nor state, that I could see,
Mair than an honest ploughman.

Then from his Lordship I shall learn,
Henceforth to meet with unconcern
One rank as weel's another;
Nae honest, worthy man need care
To meet with noble youthful Daer,
For he but meets a brother.

On November 27, 1786, Burns, riding a borrowed pony, left Mossgiel for Edinburgh, sixty miles distant. At Biggar, in Lanarkshire, he broke his journey and was entertained by a farmer acquaintance. He reached Edinburgh on the 29th, and, happening to meet a west-countryman proceeding home, asked him to return the pony to the owner. The proceeds of the Kilmarnock edition had largely gone to pay his passage to Jamaica, so Burns was in his usual financial condition. Having sought out a Mauchline man, a clerk named Richmond who at that time rented a room at half a crown a week, Burns arranged to lodge with him, and shared his bed during the visit. For a day or two the poet wandered about Edinburgh, feasting his eyes on scenes famous in Scotland's story, many of them recalling the glorious names he himself had sung in the obscurity of his Ayrshire home. His feelings found vent in the "Address to Edinburgh," written a few days after his arrival :

> Wild beats my heart to trace your steps
> Whose ancestors, in days of yore,
> Thro' hostile ranks and ruin'd gaps
> Old Scotia's bloody lion bore :
> Ev'n I who sing in rustic lore,
> Haply my Sires have left their shed,
> And fac'd grim Danger's loudest roar,
> Bold-following where your Fathers led !

It is characteristic of Burns, this satisfying of his artistic soul first. It might be expected that he would have sought out Dr. Blacklock, whose criticism had determined him to try his fortune in the capital, but it was not until some weeks had gone by that Burns, by special invitation, called on his friendly critic, and then, as it happened, he no longer needed the proffered help. The poet entered Edinburgh a gawky, somewhat ungainly rustic, all eyes, an impudent staring fellow to outward appearance; but when it was noised abroad that this was Mr. Burns, the poet, society received him with open arms. Within a fortnight he was writing to his Ayrshire friends brief accounts of his wonderful reception. The local gentry stood loyally by their neighbour. Mr. Dalrymple, of Orangefield, introduced him to the highest social set; Dugald Stewart made him free of the best intellectual society also. A week after his arrival—on December 7, to be precise—Gavin Hamilton got all the news: "For my own affairs, I am in a fair way of becoming as eminent as Thomas à Kempis or John Bunyan; and you may expect henceforth to see my birthday inserted among the wonderful events. . . . My Lord Glencairn and the Dean of Faculty, Mr. H. Erskine, have taken me under their wing; and by all probability I shall soon be the tenth worthy, and the eighth wise man of the world. Through my lord's influence it is inserted in the records of the Caledonian Hunt that they universally, one and all, subscribe for the 2d edition. My subscription bills come out to-morrow. . . ." Six days later he informs his friend Ballantine, of Ayr, to whom he had dedicated "The Twa Brigs," that he had been introduced to a good many of the noblesse, but his avowed patrons and patronesses were the Duchess of Gordon ; the Countess of Glencairn, with my Lord, and Lady Betty ; the Dean of Faculty ; Sir John Whitefoord ; Patrick Miller, of Dalswinton. Amongst his literary friends he includes Professors Stewart and Blair, and Mr. Mackenzie—the Man of Feeling, so designated from the title of his most important work. On December 14 Creech, the leading publisher, advertised the poems as in the press, "to be published by subscription for the sole benefit of the author." In short, the success of Burns was instantaneous. He took Edinburgh by storm.

The Henry Mackenzie mentioned above was the man whose reputation as a critic stood highest in Scotland. He had just done Burns a great service. On December 9, a generous critique from his pen appeared in "The Lounger," a magazine of the Addisonian type edited by him. This, of course, was not the first favourable review Burns had received, but certainly it was the most authoritative that could be given. Mackenzie boldly pronounced the poet a genius of no ordinary rank. After quoting some stanzas from "The Vision" and all of "To a Mountain Daisy," the critic continued : "The power of genius is not less admirable in tracing the manners than in painting the passions or in drawing the scenery of Nature. That intuitive glance with which a writer like Shakespeare discerns the characters of men, with which he catches the many-changing hues of life, forms a sort of problem in the science of mind, of which it is easier to see the truth than to assign the cause. Though I am very far from meaning to compare our rustic bard to Shakespeare, yet whoever will read his lighter and more humorous poems, his Dialogue of the Dogs, his Dedication to G[avin] H[amilton], Esq., his Epistles to a Young Friend and to W[illiam] S[imson], will perceive with what uncommon penetration and sagacity this Heaven-taught ploughman, from his humble and unlettered station, has looked upon men and manners."

It is somewhat surprising to find Mackenzie anticipating the trend of modern criticism in selecting for his highest praise those genuine bursts of racy humour. The Man of Feeling was a sentimentalist of the school of Sterne, he was regarded as the acme of polite learning, in his own works he shows a staid respectability verging even on genteel smugness, he is everywhere the moralist ; but this judgment of his on Burns shows that he was no mere bookish critic and that his knowledge of life was not gained by looking at it always through sentimental glasses. Mackenzie had been one of the formative influences of Burns. The poet wore out two copies of "The Man of Feeling," carrying it about with him in his pocket to dip into at odd moments. When he drew the idyllic scene of "The Cotter's Saturday Night," when he proclaimed his boundless love of mankind in "The Twa Dogs," when he showed his large-hearted sensibility in "To a Mouse," when he sympathised with the poor outcast creatures in "The Jolly Beggars" and offered even the devil a crumb of comfort in "The Address to the Deil," when he luxuriated in his own grief as in "The Dirge" and "Despondency," Burns showed himself the true child of his age and gave his own powerful expression to eighteenth-century commonplaces. Thus as a sentimentalist he had a distinct claim on Mackenzie, but there was a danger that the daring originality and racy humour of Burns might not be favoured by the critic.

The year 1787 was one of Burns's lean years. Balls, masques, dinners, breakfasts, claret parties, masonic meetings, drinking clubs, social conviviality in all its forms and gradations, these checked the flow of genius. Of the poems said to have been composed at Edinburgh only one, "To a Haggis," is of outstanding merit, and even that may have been written earlier. In the first flush of fame Burns behaved grandly. He did not run after the great: it was they who sought him out. His whole conduct at this time betokened modest independence based on conscious merit. He had come to Edinburgh not to flatter, not to curry favour, not to write to command, but to sell what he had already written, to take his stand on his own merits, and, if fortune so far favoured him, to mingle with the great as their intellectual, and almost their social, equal. He knew his own powers, and while he was always courteous to those who offered him criticisms, he rarely accepted their judgment. Indeed, only once did he alter a single word. In this case the critic was the great Dr. Blair. What Burns thought of Blair is recorded in the commonplace book which the poet commenced to keep in Edinburgh. He regarded him as merely an astonishing proof of what industry and application could do, and as a critic of the very first rank in *Prose*. But Blair had a kind heart and was doing his best, in his superior way, so Burns humoured him on one solitary occasion. It is rather amusing to find the rustic in the privacy of his diary criticising the fine gentry whom he met. Not all the lords had the practical common sense of the Earl of Eglintoun, who, remembering that, pending the publication of the poems, Burns might need some ready cash, paid his subscription of ten guineas three months in advance. The Earl of Buchan, on the other hand, wrote that he was going to buy six copies for himself, and on the strength of this order presumed to dictate to the poet a recipe for his future greatness. Buchan's poetic counsels are of little value, but one quaintly turned sentence concerning general conduct is almost prophetic in its significance : "Keep your Eye upon Parnassus and drink deep of the fountains of Helicon, but beware of the Joy that is dedicated to the Jolly God of wine." To all such letters the bard wrote discreet replies.

Burns was violent in his likes and dislikes, and often his predilections were founded on no reasonable basis. This trait explains his extravagant love—a love almost approaching worship—of James, Earl of Glencairn. This nobleman was the means of getting the entire Caledonian Hunt to subscribe for the poems, and amongst his private friends he seems to have acted as a canvasser for the poet. He sent a parcel of subscription bills to the Marquis of Graham "with downright orders to get them filled up with all the first Scottish names at Court." But others had done equally well. The real secret of Glencairn's influence over Burns was his personal charm and his good heart. He treated Burns, as did Lord Daer, as a man and a brother, and the poet saw that he was sincere. Burns was ever a grateful man, but the love he bore Glencairn was not merely the love of gratitude. It was the strong love of a kindred spirit.

It is characteristic of Burns that as soon as possible he sought out the grave of Fergusson, and, finding it ill kept, asked and was granted permission to put it into decent order. At his own expense he caused a simple stone suitably inscribed to be placed over the grave. In this way Burns showed his reverence for and gratitude to his predecessor. Almost at the same time a young lad who was afterwards to achieve fame as a writer was brought for a brief space to pay his homage to the ploughman-poet. Walter Scott met Burns at one of the Edinburgh salons, and in after-days used to recall the meeting with pride. The incident through which he won the praise of the poet is well known. Nasmyth, a young landscape painter, but to whom the world owes the best portrait of Burns, was at this period frequently with him, and the artist in words and the artist in colour made excursions together in the environs of the city. Of a more convivial turn, and therefore more in the night than in the day society, was William Nicol, a master in the High School. His name henceforth figures largely in Burns's correspondence. One of the last men that Burns met in Edinburgh was James Johnson, who was then engaged in collecting and publishing in "The Scots Musical Museum" many of the old favourite songs of the country-side. This appealed especially to Burns, and he at once promised Johnson all the assistance in his power. Most of Burns's subsequent songs appeared in this publication. Many years afterwards no fewer than 184 of the pieces which compose the collection were found written out in Burns's own hand.

The Edinburgh Edition came out on April 21, 1787. Its success was already assured, and having no longer anything to detain him in the capital, Burns set out for home. He went by a circuitous route, by the Border country, proceeding as far south as Newcastle before turning westward and northward. Everywhere on the journey he was made much of: was entertained by the best people; elected a free member of many masonic lodges; enrolled a freeman of several towns—and in this connection Dumfries is notable. Burns met many beautiful ladies, paid them poetic compliments, and recorded their charms in his diary. But on his return to Mauchline the old intimacy with Jean Armour was at once renewed. He was now recognised as of national importance, and the Armour household showed such a change of front that Burns was disgusted with their servility. Save for Jean, Mauchline was no longer attractive. The poet had arrived back on June 9, 1787, and a few days later he was off on his travels again. He toured in the West Highlands, came back to Mauchline towards the end of July, and proceeded again to Edinburgh early in August. The profits of the second edition were considerable, and Burns was now able to satisfy a long-cherished ambition to visit some of the most famous scenes in his country's story. Accompanied by Nichol, he set out for a long tour in the Highlands. Proceeding by Stirlingshire, Perthshire, and Inverness, he returned by Aberdeen and the east coast, and so was enabled to visit his relatives in Kincardineshire. On this tour he kept a diary which is singularly disappointing to those who have read the journals of other poets in similar circumstances. With some notable exceptions, it is the barest of itineraries ; but frequent allusions to crops, farms, and estate management indicate that the diarist looked around him with the eye of the prospecting agriculturist. As a matter of fact, he was contemplating the possibilities of his own future career. Another short tour in the Devon valley brought his journeyings to a close.

He was again in Edinburgh in September 1787, and there he remained in idleness until March 1788. This, his second lengthy stay in the capital, was very different from his first triumphant entry. He was no longer fêted and lionised by society. Indeed, he was actually cold-shouldered. Carlyle waxes eloquently indignant at this neglect of genius and mourns for the dead lion; but Burns, while he could not but be aware of the changed manner of many of his fine friends, seems to have resigned himself to it with philosophic cheerfulness. Perhaps he himself was to blame. Doubtless he made some mistakes of the grosser sort, and on occasion may have scandalised the gossips. A good deal of tittle-tattle began to be circulated about him, and from this time on till his death he was much distressed by and strove to defend himself against the slander which imputed drunkenness to him. Burns in his cups certainly was guilty of some indiscretions, but the rarity of these occasions seems to have added to rather than lessened the enormity of such offences, which, after all, were those of his age. No man grieved so much over his shortcomings: no man suffered so keenly the pangs of remorse. Even in this he displays true nobility of soul.

Burns at first had no intention of spending so much time in Edinburgh. His chief business there was to settle accounts with Creech, the publisher of the second edition. The profits of the publication are variously estimated from £400 to £700, but Creech had to be dunned for the money. He kept Burns off with fair promises, and it was only after two years had elapsed that he gave the poet his final payment. Another cause contributed to Burns's enforced idleness. He had the misfortune to break his leg, and was laid up for several months. During this time he began a remarkable correspondence with Mrs. McLehose, a pretty and witty young lady, the wife of a planter in the West Indies. This correspondence has now been published in full, and it adds to the mystery of Burns. Carried on in the most romantic manner by the poet under the pseudonym of Sylvander and by the lady as Clarinda, if sincere it is certainly one of the most remarkable intrigues even in the loves of poets, and if artificial it is surely the most wonderful game of make-believe ever played. Some of Burns's best verses celebrate Clarinda.

In March 1788 the poet was well enough to leave Edinburgh. He felt that the life he led there was fast demoralising him, and therefore he was much concerned to get some settled employment. Several avenues were open to him: he might support himself by literary work; he might try farming again; he might secure a Government appointment from his influential friends. Burns could not bring himself to write deliberately for gain, and he felt that he must have some certainty of maintenance apart altogether from writing. Nevertheless he determined that in whatever calling he should pursue there must be leisure for poetry. An official appointment might meet the case. Quite early in his career Burns had thought of the Excise as a suitable vocation, but his gorge had risen at the thought of spending his life gauging beer-barrels. But the salary of a Collector in the Excise ranged from £300 to £800 and the duties were comparatively light, and if rapid promotion could be ensured it was worth while to perform the drudgery of the lower grades. With influential backing Burns believed that a Collectorship was easily within his reach. He therefore asked his friends, the Earl of Glencairn and Mr. Graham, of Fintry, to nominate him in case he should decide to enter the Government service. When he left Edinburgh he carried with him an Excise commission which on presentation to the authorities would ensure him employment, but he was resolved to make use of it only as a last resort. The most attractive prospect of all was that of farming. He was now in possession of sufficient capital to stock a farm which would guarantee him a livelihood. He would be his own master and have leisure to write. "A life of literary leisure with a decent competency," he says in one of his letters, "is the summit of my wishes." Having debated thus in his mind for many months, he determined to try farming, and if that should fail, to fall back upon the Excise.

Leaving Edinburgh, and breaking off his intercourse with Clarinda, he hied him to Mauchline, and there, shortly after, espoused Jean Armour. Burns had had many romantic attachments, but there is no doubt that Jean was the lass that he loved best. He never regretted his choice. She understood his nature thoroughly and proved a loyal and sympathetic wife. After having been offered a choice of several farms by an Edinburgh patron, Patrick Miller, of Dalswinton, he entered upon the tenancy of Ellisland, a farm beautifully situated on the banks of the Nith, six miles from Dumfries. His wife was left at Mauchline, for there was no house on the farm. He himself dwelt in a hut during the months that the house was being built, and besides the labours of the farm he also superintended the operations of the artisans. It was during this period of loneliness that he composed, in honour of his wife, the popular song, " I love my Jean."

OF A' THE AIRTS THE WIND CAN BLAW

Of a' the airts the wind can blaw,
  I dearly like the west,
For there the bonnie lassie lives,
  The lassie I lo'e best :
There wild woods grow, and rivers row,
  And mony a hill between,
But day and night my fancy's flight
  Is ever wi' my Jean.

I see her in the dewy flowers,
  I see her sweet and fair ;

I hear her in the tunefu' birds,
  I hear her charm the air :
There's not a bonnie flower that springs
  By fountain, shaw, or green,
There's not a bonnie bird that sings,
  But minds me o' my Jean.

In December 1788 he brought his young wife from Mauchline, and, observing an old Scottish custom, they entered their new home arm-in-arm, preceded by a servant carrying a Bible. This arrangement was supposed to bring good fortune, but alas ! Burns's halcyon time was of short duration. The same ill-luck dogged his footsteps. Ellisland proved a failure as a farm. Its tenant began to rue his choice, and, were it not for the underlying tragedy, the language he used in describing its sterility would provoke laughter. It was well that he had his Excise commission to fall back upon, for, in his own picturesque phrase, "the riddlings of creation"—that is, Ellisland—would soon have reduced him to beggary. In the face of starvation he no longer harboured æsthetic scruples, but very wisely presented his commission, and almost at once received an appointment as an Exciseman for the district in which his farm was situated. This was in 1789. The remuneration for the Excise work was £50 per annum, sufficient, with the farm, to keep the wolf from the door. Although Burns thought his new profession somewhat degrading for a poet, he did not shirk the unpleasant work, and in the hope of rising by sheer merit he discharged his duties with exemplary zeal. In his letters he looked forward to being a "collector" or even "surveyor-general," and it was his intention to work Ellisland as a dairy-farm till the hoped-for promotion came. Then he would give up the farm altogether, lead a more leisurely life, and devote himself to poetry. Meanwhile he found Excise work physically trying: he had the supervision of ten parishes and had to ride, on an average, and of course in all weathers, 200 miles a week. Robert Ainslie, the friend who had accompanied him on his Border journey, visited him at Ellisland and found him in a very cheery frame of mind: "Our friend is as ingenious as ever. His mind seems to me to be a great mixture of the poet and Exciseman. One day he sits down and writes a beautiful poem—and the next seizes a cargo of tobacco from some unfortunate smuggler, or roups out some poor wretch for selling liquors without a licence."

The flow of poetry of the Ellisland period, while inconsiderable compared with the wonderful flood-tide of Mossgiel, nevertheless was remarkably steady. The poet mainly busied himself with song-writing, most of his productions being published in Johnson's "Musical Museum," to which reference has already been made. Some of Burns's most famous songs were written at Ellisland. "O were I on Parnassus Hill," "McPherson's Farewell," "Auld Lang Syne," "Up in the Morning

Early," "My Bonnie Mary," "John Anderson," "My Heart's in the Highlands," "Tam Glen," "The Banks of Nith," "The Banks o' Doon," "Afton Water," are a few of those composed between the years 1788 and 1791.

AULD LANG SYNE

Should auld acquaintance be forgot,
  And never brought to min'?
Should auld acquaintance be forgot,
  And auld lang syne?

CHORUS

For auld lang syne, my dear,
  For auld lang syne,
We'll tak' a cup o' kindness yet,
  For auld lang syne!

We twa ha'e run about the brae,
  And pou'd the gowans fine;
But we've wandered mony a weary foot
  Sin' auld lang syne.
    For auld, &c.

We twa ha'e paidl'd i' the burn,
  Frae morning sun till dine;
But seas between us braid ha'e roared
  Sin' auld lang syne.
    For auld, &c.

And here's a hand, my trustie fiere,
  And gie's a hand o' thine;
And we'll tak' a right guid willie-waught,
  For auld lang syne!
    For auld, &c.

And surely ye'll be your pint-stoup,
And surely I'll be mine ;
And we'll tak' a cup o' kindness yet
For auld lang syne.
For auld, &c.

THE BANKS OF NITH

The Thames flows proudly to the sea,
Where royal cities stately stand ;
But sweeter flows the Nith to me,
Where Cummins ance had high command :
When shall I see that honour'd land,
That winding stream I love so dear ?
Must wayward fortune's adverse hand
For ever, ever keep me here ?

How lovely, Nith, thy fruitful vales,
Where spreading hawthorns gaily bloom ;
How sweetly wind thy sloping dales,
Where lambkins wander thro' the broom !
Tho' wandering, now, must be my doom,
Far from thy bonnie banks and braes,
May there my latest hours consume,
Amang my friends of early days !

THE BANKS O' DOON

Ye banks and braes o' bonnie Doon,
How can ye bloom sae fresh and fair ?
How can ye chant, ye little birds,
And I sae weary, fu' o' care !
Thou'll break my heart, thou warbling bird,
That wantons through the flowering thorn !
Thou minds me o' departed joys,
Departed—never to return !

Oft ha'e I roved by bonnie Doon,
To see the rose and woodbine twine ;
And ilka bird sang o' its luve,
And fondly sae did I o' mine.
Wi' lightsome heart I pu'd a rose,
Fu' sweet upon its thorny tree ;
And my fause lover stole my rose,
But, ah ! he left the thorn wi' me.

AFTON WATER

Flow gently, sweet Afton, among thy green braes,
Flow gently, I'll sing thee a song in thy praise ;
My Mary's asleep by thy murmuring stream,—
Flow gently, sweet Afton, disturb not her dream.

Thou stock-dove, whose echo resounds through the glen,
Ye wild whistling blackbirds in yon thorny den,
Thou green-crested lapwing thy screaming forbear,—
I charge you, disturb not my slumbering fair !

How lofty, sweet Afton, thy neighbouring hills,
Far-marked with the courses of clear-winding rills !
There daily I wander, as noon rises high,
My flocks and my Mary's sweet cot in my eye.

How pleasant thy banks and green valleys below,
Where wild in the woodlands the primroses blow ;
There oft as mild evening weeps over the lea,
The sweet-scented birk shades my Mary and me.

Thy crystal stream, Afton, how lovely it glides,
And winds by the cot where my Mary resides ;
How wanton thy waters her snawy feet lave,
As gath'ring sweet flowerets, she stems thy clear wave !

Flow gently, sweet Afton, among thy green braes,
Flow gently, sweet river, the theme of my lays ;
My Mary's asleep by thy murmuring stream,—
Flow gently, sweet Afton, disturb not her dream !

On Burns's settling in Dumfriesshire his company was much sought after by the neighbouring gentry, and the poet was the life and soul of many merry meetings. His chief associate was an immediate neighbour, Captain Riddel of Glenriddel. For this gentleman he copied out many of his unpublished poems. These now constitute the Glenriddel manuscript. At Friar's Carse, the home of the gallant captain, took place a great drinking bout between three Nithsdale gentlemen, the prize being a small ebony whistle said to have been brought to Scotland by a Danish gentleman in the train of Anne of Denmark, wife of James the Sixth. Burns celebrated the contest in a ballad of no particular interest. An episode of a similar nature, but in which the poet took a more active part, happened at Moffat in the autumn of 1789, and gave rise to what has been called the best Bacchanalian song ever written, "Willie brew'd a Peck o' Maut." Burns gave the following account of its origin in a brief note in the "Musical Museum" : "This air is Masterton's ; the song mine. The occasion of it was this. Mr. Wm. Nicol of the High School, Edinburgh, during the autumn vacation being at Moffat, honest Allan, who was at that time on a visit to Dalswinton, and I went to pay

Nicol a visit. We had such a joyous meeting that Mr. Masterton and I agreed, each in our own way, that we should celebrate the business."

WILLIE BREW'D A PECK O' MAUT

O, Willie brew'd a peck o' maut,
  And Rob and Allan cam' to see ;
Three blither hearts, that lee lang night,
  Ye wad na found in Christendie.

CHORUS

We are na fou, we're nae that fou,
  But just a drappie in our e'e !
The cock may craw, the day may daw',
  And ay we'll taste the barley bree !

Here are we met, three merry boys,
  Three merry boys, I trow, are we ;
And mony a night we've merry been,
  And mony mae we hope to be !

It is the moon—I ken her horn,
  That's blinkin' in the lift sae hie ;
She shines sae bright to wyle us hame,
  But, by my sooth, she'll wait a wee !

Wha first shall rise to gang awa',
  A cuckold, coward loon is he !
Wha last beside his chair shall fa',
  He is the king amang us three !

We are na fou, we're nae that fou,
  But just a drappie in our e'e ;
The cock may craw, the day may daw',
  And ay we'll taste the barley bree.

Burns was largely a man of moods, and it is but natural that these moods should be reflected in his poetry. The *volte face* from gay to grave is strikingly exemplified in a pathetic love-lyric which, though it seems almost incredible, was composed at the same time as the above " swaggering upspring reel." Mary Campbell had died in 1786, and the third anniversary of her death had come. Her memory was dear to Burns—but let Jean tell the story in her own words: " When the gloaming came, he grew sad about something : he could not rest. He wandered first up the water-side, and then went to the barnyard ; and I followed him, begging him to come in, as he was ill, and the air was cold and sharp. He always promised, but still remained where he was, striding up and down, and looking at the clear sky, and particularly at a star that shone like another moon." When at last Burns entered the house he called for ink and paper and transcribed the following verses:

TO MARY IN HEAVEN

Thou lingering star, with lessening ray,
  That lov'st to greet the early morn,
Again thou usher'st in the day
  My Mary from my soul was torn.
O Mary ! dear departed shade !
  Where is thy place of blissful rest ?
Seest thou thy lover lowly laid ?
  Hear'st thou the groans that rend his breast ?

That sacred hour can I forget?
  Can I forget the hallowed grove,
Where, by the winding Ayr, we met,
  To live one day of parting love?
Eternity will not efface
  Those records dear of transports past;
Thy image at our last embrace—
  Ah, little thought we 'twas our last!

Ayr, gurgling, kissed his pebbled shore,
  O'erhung with wild woods, thickening green;
The fragrant birch, and hawthorn hoar,
  Twined am'rous round the raptured scene;
The flowers sprang wanton to be prest,
  The birds sang love on every spray—
Till too, too soon the glowing west,
  Proclaimed the speed of wingèd day.

Still o'er these scenes my mem'ry wakes,
  And fondly broods with miser care!
Time but th' impression stronger makes,
  As streams their channels deeper wear.
My Mary, dear departed shade!
  Where is thy place of blissful rest?
Seest thou thy lover lowly laid?
  Hear'st thou the groans that rend his breast?

It is noticeable that some of Burns's most serious pieces are written largely in English—witness "Man was made to mourn," parts of "The Cotter's Saturday Night," and "To Mary in Heaven." In his songs, too, he deliberately picked and chose those Scotch words which he thought would add to the musical effect and were otherwise suitable to the theme. If one tries to substitute the English forms of these words one finds that, though the metre in most cases remains unaltered, there is still some loss of charm. Burns boldly claimed musical superiority for the dialect, and in his letters to his publisher always insisted on being allowed "a sprinkling of Scotch words." On the other hand, in his humorous poems Burns made a full use of Scotch, and in this connection it is well to remember that much of the dialect was really a survival of the older literary forms, and, though understood, was not really the speech either of Burns or of his contemporaries.

In 1790 the poet, all his life of a mercurial temperament, was growing more and more despondent. The cares of a growing family began to weigh heavy upon him, and he feared for the future. Nevertheless to this year belongs the merry tale of "Tam o' Shanter." At Friar's Carse the poet met an English antiquary, by name Captain Grose, who was travelling in Scotland in order to secure material for a book, "The Antiquities of Scotland." The antiquary was a witty, good-natured, funny little man, and Burns and he became great friends. Burns asked him to include an account of Alloway Kirk in his book, and the antiquary promised to do so if the poet would provide some verses to accompany an engraving of the ruin. Burns fulfilled the condition in a most startling manner by producing, not a few verses, but a long poem. It was composed on a single day in the fields, and was written out by the poet—with the top of a sod dyke for a desk! Burns used to revel in this poem, and always affirmed that it was his best work.

TAM O' SHANTER

When chapman billies leave the street
And drouthy neebors neebors meet,
As market-days are wearing late,
An' folk begin to tak' the gate;
While we sit bousing at the nappy,
An' getting fou and unco happy,
We think na on the lang Scots miles,
The mosses, waters, slaps, and stiles,
That lie between us and our hame,
Whare sits our sulky, sullen dame,
Gathering her brows like gathering storm,
Nursing her wrath to keep it warm.

This truth fand honest Tam o' Shanter,
As he frae Ayr ae night did canter,
(Auld Ayr, wham ne'er a town surpasses,
For honest men and bonny lasses.)

O Tam! hadst thou but been sae wise,
As ta'en thy ain wife Kate's advice!
She tauld thee weel thou was a skellum,
A blethering, blustering, drunken blellum,
That frae November till October,
Ae market-day thou was nae sober;
That ilka melder, wi' the miller,
Thou sat as lang as thou had siller;

That every naig was ca'd a shoe on,
The smith and thee gat roaring fou on ;
That at the Lord's house, ev'n on Sunday,
Thou drank wi' Kirkton Jean till Monday.
She prophesied that, late or soon,
Thou would be found deep drowned in Doon ;
Or catched wi' warlocks in the mirk,
By Alloway's auld haunted kirk.

Ah, gentle dames ! it gars me greet,
To think how mony counsels sweet,
How many lengthened sage advices,
The husband frae the wife despises !

But to our tale : Ae market-night,
Tam had got planted unco right ;
Fast by an ingle bleezing finely,
Wi' reaming swats, that drank divinely ;
And at his elbow, Souter Johnny,
His ancient, trusty, drouthy crony ;
Tam lo'ed him like a vera brither ;
They had been fou for weeks thegither.
The night drave on wi' sangs an' clatter ;
And aye the ale was growing better :
The landlady and Tam grew gracious,
Wi' favours, secret, sweet, and precious :
The Souter tauld his queerest stories ;
The landlord's laugh was ready chorus :
The storm without might rair and rustle,
Tam did na mind the storm a whistle.
Care, mad to see a man sae happy,
E'en drowned himself amang the nappy ;
As bees flee hame wi' lades o' treasure,
The minutes winged their way wi' pleasure
Kings may be blest, but Tam was glorious,
O'er a' the ills o' life victorious !

But pleasures are like poppies spread,
You seize the flower, its bloom is shed!
Or like the snow-fall in the river,
A moment white—then melts for ever;
Or like the borealis race,
That flit ere you can point their place;
Or like the rainbow's lovely form
Evanishing amid the storm.

Nae man can tether time or tide;
The hour approaches Tam maun ride;
That hour, o' night's black arch the keystane.
That dreary hour he mounts his beast in;
And sic a night he tak's the road in,
As ne'er poor sinner was abroad in.
The wind blew as 'twad blawn its last;
The rattlin' showers rose on the blast:
The speedy gleams the darkness swallowed;
Loud, deep, and lang the thunder bellowed;
That night, a child might understand,
The De'il had business on his hand.

Weel mounted on his grey mare, Meg,
(A better never lifted leg,)
Tam skelpit on through dub and mire,
Despising wind, and rain, and fire;
Whiles holding fast his guid blue bonnet;
Whiles crooning o'er some auld Scots sonnet;
Whiles glow'ring round wi' prudent cares,
Lest bogles catch him unawares;
Kirk-Alloway was drawing nigh,
Whare ghaists and houlets nightly cry.

By this time he was cross the ford,
Whare in the snaw the chapman smoored;

And past the birks and meikle stane,
Whare drunken Charlie brak's neck-bane ,
And through the whins, and by the cairn,
Whare hunters fand the murdered bairn ;
And near the thorn, aboon the well,
Whare Mungo's mither hanged hersel'.
Before him Doon pours all his floods ;
The doubling storm roars through the woods !
The lightnings flash from pole to pole ;
Near and more near the thunders roll ;
When, glimmering through the groaning trees,
Kirk-Alloway seemed in a bleeze ;
Through ilka bore the beams were glancing ;
And loud resounded mirth and dancing.

Inspiring, bold John Barleycorn !
What dangers thou canst mak' us scorn !
Wi' tippenny we fear nae evil ;
Wi' usquabae we'll face the Devil !
The swats sae reamed in Tammie's noddle,
Fair play, he cared na de'ils a boddle.
But Maggie stood right sair astonished,
Till, by the heel and hand admonished,
She ventured forward on the light ;
And, wow ! Tam saw an unco sight !
Warlocks and witches in a dance ;
Nae cotillon brent new frae France,
But hornpipes, jigs, strathspeys, and reels,
Put life and mettle in their heels.
At winnock-bunker in the east,
There sat Auld Nick, in shape o' beast ;
A towzie tyke, black, grim, and large,
To gi'e them music was his charge :
He screwed the pipes and gart them skirl,
Till roof and rafters a' did dirl !

Coffins stood round, like open presses,
That shawed the dead in their last dresses;
And by some devilish cantrip sleight,
Each in its cauld hand held a light,
By which heroic Tam was able
To note upon the haly table,
A murderer's banes in gibbet airns ;
Twa span-lang, wee unchristened bairns ;
A thief new-cutted frae a rape,
Wi' his last gasp his gab did gape :
Five tomahawks, wi' bluid red-rusted ;
Five scimitars wi' murder crusted ;
A garter, which a babe had strangled ;
A knife, a father's throat had mangled,
Whom his ain son o' life bereft,
The grey hairs yet stack to the heft ;
Wi' mair o' horrible and awfu',
Which ev'n to name wad be unlawfu'.

As Tammie glowred, amazed and curious,
The mirth and fun grew fast and furious :
The piper loud and louder blew ;
The dancers quick and quicker flew ;
They reeled, they set, they crossed, they cleekit,
Till ilka carlin swat and reekit,
And coost her duddies to the wark,
And linket at it in her sark !

Now Tam, O Tam ! had they been queans
A' plump and strapping, in their teens ;
Their sarks, instead o' creeshie flannen,
Been snaw-white seventeen hunder linen ;
Thir breeks o' mine, my only pair,
That ance were plush, o' guid blue hair,
I wad hae gi'en them off my hurdies,
For ane blink o' the bonnie burdies !

But withered beldams old and droll,
Rigwoodie hags wad spean a foal,
Lowping and flinging on a crummock,
I wonder didna turn thy stomach.

But Tam kenned what was what fu' brawlie
"There was ae winsome wench and walie,"
That night enlisted in the core,
(Lang after kenned on Carrick shore!
For mony a beast to dead she shot,
And perished mony a bonnie boat,
And shook baith meikle corn and bear,
And kept the country-side in fear,)
Her cutty sark, o' Paisley harn,
That while a lassie she had worn,
In longitude though sorely scanty,
It was her best, and she was vauntie.
Ah! little kenned thy reverend grannie,
That sark she coft for her wee Nannie,
Wi' twa pund Scots ('twas a' her riches,)
Wad ever graced a dance of witches!

But here my muse her wing maun cour;
Sic flights are far beyond her power:
To sing how Nannie lap and flang,
(A souple jade she was and strang,)
And how Tam stood, like ane bewitched,
And thought his very een enriched;
Even Satan glowred, and fidged fu' fain,
And hotched and blew wi' might and main;
Till first ae caper, syne anither,
Tam tint his reason a'thegither,
And roars out, "Weel done, Cutty-sark!"
And in an instant all was dark:
And scarcely had he Maggie rallied,
When out the hellish legion sallied.

As bees bizz out wi' angry fyke,
When plundering herds assail their byke ;
As open pussie's mortal foes
When, pop ! she starts before their nose ;
As eager runs the market-crowd,
When "Catch the thief ! " resounds aloud ;
So Maggie runs, the witches follow,
Wi' mony an eldritch screech and hollow.

Ah, Tam ! ah, Tam ! thou'll get thy fairin' !
In hell they'll roast thee like a herrin' !
In vain thy Kate awaits thy comin' !
Kate soon will be a woefu' woman !
Now, do thy speedy utmost, Meg,
And win the key-stane of the brig ;
There at them thou thy tail may toss,
A running stream they dare na cross.
But ere the key-stane she could make,
The fient a tail she had to shake !

For Nannie, far before the rest,
Hard upon noble Maggie prest,
And flew at Tam wi' furious ettle ;
But little wist she Maggie's mettle—
Ae spring brought off her master hale,
But left behind her ain grey tail :
The carlin claught her by the rump,
And left poor Maggie scarce a stump !

Now, wha this tale o' truth shall read,
Ilk man and mother's son, take heed :
Whene'er to drink you are inclined,
Or cutty-sarks run in your mind,
Think, ye may buy the joys o'er dear,
Remember Tam o' Shanter's mare.

A study of the letters which Burns wrote from Ellisland alone will reveal much. The extent of this correspondence, its scope of topic, its variety of style, its extraordinary biographic interest both as a record of mind and a revelation of character, cannot be regarded as other than astonishing; and more especially is this the case when it is considered as the output of a man who to the workaday world around him must have appeared as more Exciseman than farmer and more farmer than poet. The mere enumeration of his correspondents shows that he had sounded the whole gamut of society from low to high—from the jolly beggars at Poosie Nansie's to the pedantic littérateurs of the Edinburgh salons. With marvellous ability he could adapt himself to the social status of the recipients of his letters. He wrote to the nobility: to my lord duke and the most noble earl; to the territorial magnate and the humblest bonnet laird; to men of religion, from the Roman Catholic Bishop Geddes to the Calvinist minister the Reverend John McMath; to men of learning, from Dugald Stewart, professor in the University of Edinburgh, down to Murdoch, professor of the French language, alias coaching drudge, in London; to men of law—Aiken, Hamilton, Ainslie, advocates, writers to the Signet, or mere notaries public; to men of letters—Dr. Moore, the novelist, Drs. Blair and Blacklock, poets and critics, Sillar and Lapraik, poetasters; and, above all, to women, ladies old and young—the motherly Mrs. Dunlop, the sensible Margaret Chalmers, the sentimental Clarinda, my Lady Betty Cunningham, and my Lady Winifred Maxwell Constance. All this, of course, necessitated a multiplicity of subjects and a multiplicity of manners, grave and gay, coarse and refined, formal and familiar. The variety of style in these letters has led to conflicting estimates regarding Burns's prose, but the balance of opinion has been to condemn it as being highly artificial and as having all the pomp and strut and fustian of eighteenth-century polite learning. Undoubtedly the rant of extravagant youth is not absent. Burns, be it remembered, formed his prose style on a collection of elegant letters by the wits of Queen Anne's reign, and therefore during his apprenticeship employed the stilts of studied composition; but later he walked firmly on his own legs. His prose is certainly not the stock prose of the eighteenth century. Even at its worst it bears the stamp of his own powerful personality, and, for the biography of the poet, it is even more valuable than his poetry. Burns's letters are intensely human documents: there he has revealed his own frailties and the great complexity of his character. It is by studying them in the bulk that a sympathetic critic like the late Auguste Angellier is enabled in his great critical account of Burns "to give to things their immense complexity, their inexplicable confusion and their apparent contradictions."

In November 1791 the poet, taking advantage

of a change in proprietorship to break his lease and to sell off his effects, was enabled to leave Ellisland. The sale was a particularly good one and provided him with a money surplus when all accounts were settled. Having been promoted to a better post in the neighbouring town of Dumfries, he removed to a house in Bank Vennel there. His income was increased by £20 per annum, and he also had a share of the fines, seizures, &c., while his expenditure was decreased through his not having to keep a horse. His average income was thus brought up to about £100 a year, and in those days, the purchasing power of money being greater than it is now, it was possible to live comfortably enough on that sum. Leaving Ellisland was an important step for Burns. It marks his determination to rely solely on the Excise for the betterment of his worldly affairs. And as things stood in 1791 there was every probability of his gaining a supervisorship very shortly. For a time nothing disturbed these good prospects : even without political or social influence Burns in course of time would have received automatic promotion to a position which would have placed him beyond financial worry. On January 27, 1791, his name was listed as one of those recommended for the post of examiner and supervisor ; in April 1792 he obtained a small promotion ; in 1794 he acted as temporary supervisor. These appointments were all in the usual course, and are quoted to show that Burns's case was not so desperate as is commonly made out. The poet himself was of a free and generous nature with money, but his wife was a prudent manager, and had health remained with Burns all might have been well. The death of his patron, the Earl of Glencairn, may also have lessened his chances of rapid promotion, but although the poet pays him an extravagant tribute in the "Elegy on Glencairn," that nobleman's patronage was not, strictly speaking, required.

When Burns removed to Dumfries he began to take an active part in the politics of the day, and, his principles being commonly misunderstood, he brought upon himself much sorrow thereby. It was the beginning of the Revolutionary epoch in France, and to help the French patriots was at first a popular proceeding. Burns shared in that delight in the new principles which was felt by all the ardent spirits—by Wordsworth, Coleridge, Southey, to mention only literary men. He bought for a trifling sum four small pieces of ordnance, called carronades, and forthwith dispatched them as a present to the French Assembly. But the guns did not reach Dover until some months afterwards, and the relations between France and Britain having become strained in the interim, the export of this war material was prohibited. Burns's action was not officially regarded as unpatriotic or treasonable, and no formal notice of it was taken. Nevertheless he was privately reprimanded by his superior, and some of the ultra-loyalists of Dumfries began to regard him as a traitor to his country. This suspicion caused Burns much misery. Here it was Burns's temperament that was at fault. He had no fixed party views, and detested politics and politicians in the ordinary sense. With a sentimental attachment to the exiled Stewarts he might be labelled Tory; sharing the opinions of Glencairn and Erskine, he wore the blue and yellow colours of Fox, and might therefore be called Whig. For a time, on the matter of the Regency Bill, he was a Pittite, and as such opposed to Fox; yet on the king's recovery he characterised the thanksgiving service as "a solemn farce of pageant mummery." As late as 1789, writing to Mrs. Dunlop, he proclaimed himself a Jacobite. Then he became a convert to the views of Tom Paine, whose book "The Rights of Man" he presented to the Dumfries Library. He was an advocate of parliamentary reform, and wrote election ballads favouring the side which supported it. In December 1792 he wrote to Mrs. Dunlop saying he would not commit himself openly to any party, and for the sake of his family would be very careful; yet that same month he implored Graham of Fintry to save him from dismissal. In 1793, writing to the same gentleman to clear himself of the charge of disloyalty, he asserted that he was not a republican but a constitutionalist, and that he detested the action of the French Revolutionaries. Again, when France threatened to invade Britain Burns enrolled himself as a member of the

Dumfries Volunteers, raised in the general scheme to defend the country, and his martial songs did more to rouse the patriotic fervour of his countrymen than all the eloquence of Pitt and Dundas. Finally, in a letter to Erskine, the famous advocate, he gave a reasoned exposition of his political opinions, which is simply an eloquent plea against corruption. In his later years he definitely identified himself with the Whigs, and it is apparent that he hoped that they would carry the country. In his last illness he wrote some remarkable ballads for his side, and it is clear from his letters that up to within a few weeks of his death he was thinking how his official promotion might be accelerated by political intervention.

These apparent inconsistencies did not spring from a lack of principle, but rather from a superfluity of it. Throughout it all Burns was absolutely sincere; he was intellectually honest; in spite of little personal prejudices he preserved an open mind; he was really above all party. If he had been a selfish time-server he might have joined the party of Dundas, the great dispenser of patronage in Scotland; had he even stood aloof from politics he might have received preferment through social influence alone. But, conscious of his merits and with a spirit too proud to stoop to sycophancy, he was never able to conceal his convictions under the mask of indifference, and therefore spoke out on any particular question as his heart prompted him. Sectarianism, the accentuation of petty differences, he always detested. Class distinctions were hateful to him. Infringement of individual rights he narrowly scanned. His attitude in these matters receives its best expression in "A Man's a Man for a' that," written in 1795. It is an attack, a wonderfully trenchant, albeit poetic, attack on cant and snobbery: a cry for real manliness; an optimistic clarion cry sounded from the heights of hope. The doctrine and the aspiration alike command acceptance. The very diction is of wonderful terseness and simplicity.

A MAN'S A MAN FOR A' THAT

Is there, for honest poverty,
  That hangs his head, and a' that;
The coward-slave, we pass him by,
  We dare be poor for a' that!
For a' that, and a' that,
  Our toil's obscure, and a' that;
The rank is but the guinea's stamp,
  The man's the gowd for a' that.

What though on hamely fare we dine,
  Wear hoddin grey, and a' that;
Gi'e fools their silks, and knaves their wine,
  A man's a man for a' that;
For a' that, and a' that,
  Their tinsel show, and a' that;
The honest man, though e'er sae poor,
  Is king o' men for a' that.

Ye see yon birkie, ca'd a lord,
  Wha struts, and stares, and a' that;
Though hundreds worship at his word,
  He's but a coof for a' that:
For a' that, and a' that,
  His riband, star, and a' that:
The man of independent mind,
  He looks and laughs at a' that.

A prince can mak' a belted knight,
  A marquis, duke, and a' that;
But an honest man's aboon his might—
  Guid faith he mauna fa' that!
For a' that, and a' that,
  Their dignities, and a' that,
The pith o' sense and pride o' worth
  Are higher ranks than a' that.

Then let us pray that come it may,
  As come it will for a' that,
That sense and worth, o'er a' the earth,
  May bear the gree, and a' that.
For a' that, and a' that,
  It's coming yet, for a' that,
That man to man, the warld o'er,
  Shall brothers be for a' that.

The idolaters of Burns would assert that the teaching in "A Man's a Man for a' that" marks a new departure in the conception of individual liberty; and within narrow limits this may be so. But Leslie Stephen, in his monumental review of English thought, has shown beyond all cavil that for two or three generations preceding Burns the same sentiments and the same general cry for freedom were the leading features of English philosophic writing; and therefore Burns's poetry really stands at the end, and not at the beginning, of a movement. Burns is nowhere a profound thinker. He is not a pioneer. But he has keen insight and a fine selective faculty which betrays itself in the bare simplicity of his diction. His greatest gift is a genius for expression. Thus he gives to old dogma all the charm of novelty; and here he shows himself the pupil of Pope's critical precepts; he is the great exemplar of "what oft was thought, but ne'er so well exprest." Most of his longer poems followed models, but these they as far surpass as the plays of Shakespeare surpass the sources from which they were taken. Even in his songs there is the same tendency to build upon another's foundation. Sometimes a stanza, sometimes a line, sometimes only a name, shows his indebtedness to the past. And a comparison of Burns's songs with their originals at once establishes the superiority of the Ayrshire poet.

Lest all this should seem to detract from the genius of Burns and to degrade him to a mere man of talent, let the explanation be at once set forth. Burns's later literary activity displayed itself in the collecting and arranging of the old Scotch songs. In this he presents a contrast to Sir Walter Scott, whose first labour it was. Much of the old Scots minstrelsy owes its preservation to these two great poets. Burns's enthusiasm was such that if he heard a beggar in the street singing an unfamiliar song he would note the words and, if he could, the air. His own contributions to Johnson's "Musical Museum" have been already noticed. Shortly before he left Ellisland he had entered into a correspondence with Mr. George Thomson, of Edinburgh, a collector and publisher of songs, and now he exerted himself not only to make that publication representative of Scottish song-craft, but also to touch up and purify such old airs as either from the artistic or from the moral point of view stood in need of editorial treatment. He could not suffer anything to leave his hands which would tarnish the honour or poetic reputation of his country. In sending his contributions to Thomson he often enclosed a mass of song-lore and criticism many times the bulk of the original manuscript, and no one who reads these letters can fail to note the unselfish spirit in which he sacrificed his time and his own poetic gifts in order to make presentable some old ballad or to preserve in a new setting some happy phrase of the "auld makaris." A slight idea of Burns's attitude towards the undertaking may be gathered from his reply to Thomson's first letter. The request ran thus: "For the honour of Caledonia I would fain hope the writer of 'The Cotter's Saturday Night' may be induced to take up the pen. If so, we shall be able to present the public with a collection infinitely more interesting than any that has yet appeared." Burns replied: "As the request you make me will positively add to my enjoyments in complying with it, I shall enter into your undertaking with all the small proportion of abilities I have, strained to their utmost by the impulse of enthusiasm. Only don't hurry me. . . . In the honest enthusiasm with which I embark on your undertaking, to talk of money, wages, fee, hire, &c., would be downright prostitution of soul. A proof of each of the songs that I shall compose or amend I shall receive as a favour. In the rustic phrase of the season, 'Gude speed the wark.' "

To this labour of love Burns devoted the best of his poetic energies during a period of four or five years, from about 1790 to his death. The songs must not be regarded as in any sense task-work, for the poet would not tie himself down to work under contract. He was offered a post on the staff of a London newspaper, and refused it because he considered poetry as too sacred to be trafficked in. Nevertheless what he would not do himself he could freely advise others to undertake: worldliness in theory and unworldliness in practice is the great contradiction in his life. He could never write unless he were stirred to the depths of his being. In him the lyrical impulse is at its strongest, the personal note at its highest. Just as Shakespeare—were it not for the "Sonnets"—is the most impersonal of all poets, so Burns represents the triumph of pure personality, of the simple and the sensuous. It is difficult to pluck the heart out of Shakespeare's mystery, everywhere the clues are intangible and uncertain. With Burns it is equally difficult, but from another cause; the clues are provokingly numerous and real. Which of these many loose ends must be seized upon to lead into the labyrinth of his character? One thread seems to run straight and true, but then it winds and doubles, criss-crosses with other threads, and finally loses itself in a tangled skein which the best, the most dexterous fingers in the world can only partially unravel. Nevertheless up to a certain point the way is always clear, the poet's life is everywhere elucidated by his poetry. Everything he wrote is based on personal experience and therefore rings true. And this is so even where he shows indebtedness to his predecessors. The whole spirit of the past seems to enter into his nature; he becomes "saturate with its tradition, absolute master of its emotions and effects."

Consider how his songs were produced. An impressionable boy entering upon his teens, he hears a harvest lass singing in the field, and composes a song in her honour to the selfsame tune she sings. A country lad new come to man's estate, his heart throbs out its ecstasy of passion in the exquisite lyric dedicated to the lovely Mary Morison. In a golden moment he encounters a lovely, haughty lady of high degree strolling in the woods of Ballochmyle, and henceforth by his genius she is married to immortal verse. Recognised as a poet of national celebrity, he tours through the classic scenes of his native land, and wherever his gaze rests in approbation he transfigures and transmutes that scene with divinest alchemy : the winding Nith, Gala Water, the banks o' Doon, the birks of Aberfeldy, Castle Gordon, become exquisite and rare. He visits a battlefield, the wailing of women is borne down upon him from afar, and the lovely Lass o' Inverness rises in his fancy. He rides through a tempest on a wild Galloway moor, and while battling with the elements imagines himself at Bannockburn ; he sees the serried ranks of the Scots, how they stand firm against the shock of English spears, and then he raises the pæan of triumph, "Scots wha hae." Lonely on his Nithsdale farm, his mind reverts to the scenes of his former home, and he breathes to the young wife he has left in Ayrshire the tenderest and most delicate of his love-lyrics, "I love my Jean." Forgathering with his cronies, he is seized with the spirit of conviviality, and in a flash bursts forth with that swaggering Bacchanalian ditty, "Willie brew'd a Peck o' Maut." Struck with a chance phrase in a friend's letter, he overflows with kindly emotion, and there wells up in him a song of comfort and happy memories, "Auld Lang Syne." Obsessed by his official duties, and cursing the dilatoriness of his subordinate sent to fetch the dragoons to aid in the capture of a stranded smuggling craft, he loses his anger in mirth and whiles away the time by blaming the deil—a very pied piper of a deil—in that humorous lilt, "The Deil's awa wi' the

Exciseman." A dear friend is about to depart for the West Indies: he hastens to her, and in the sorrow of parting there is distilled that quintessence of emotion, "Ae Fond Kiss." In his last sad years, pressed with the load of life, he sees a lovely blue-eyed maiden, and at once enrols himself a votary at the shrine of beauty and celebrates the fair Chloris with songs of platonic love. And, choose where you will, so it is with all Burns's songs. A little spark sets the tinder ablaze.

A RED, RED ROSE

O, my luve's like a red, red rose,
That's newly sprung in June:
O, my luve's like the melodie
That's sweetly played in tune.

As fair art thou, my bonnie lass,
So deep in luve am I;
And I will luve thee still, my dear,
Till a' the seas gang dry.

Till a' the seas gang dry, my dear,
And the rocks melt wi' the sun!
I will luve thee still, my dear,
While the sands o' life shall run.

And fare thee weel, my only luve!
And fare thee weel a while!
And I will come again, my luve,
Though it were ten thousand mile!

AE FOND KISS

Ae fond kiss, and then we sever ;
Ae fareweel, and then, for ever !
Deep in heart-wrung tears I'll pledge thee,
Warring sighs and groans I'll wage thee.
Who shall say that Fortune grieves him,
While the star of hope she leaves him ?
Me, nae cheerfu' twinkle lights me ;
Dark despair around benights me.

I'll ne'er blame my partial fancy,
Naething could resist my Nancy ;
But to see her was to love her ;
Love but her, and love for ever.
Had we never loved sae kindly,
Had we never loved sae blindly,
Never met—or never parted,
We had ne'er been broken-hearted.

Fare thee weel, thou first and fairest !
Fare thee weel, thou best and dearest !
Thine be ilka joy and treasure,
Peace, enjoyment, love, and pleasure !
Ae fond kiss, and then we sever ;
Ae farewell, alas ! for ever !
Deep in heart-wrung tears I'll pledge thee,
Warring sighs and groans I'll wage thee !

WHEN I THINK ON THE HAPPY DAYS

When I think on the happy days
  I spent wi' you, my dearie ;
And now what lands between us lie,
  How can I be but eerie !

How slow ye move, ye heavy hours,
   As ye were wae and weary !
It was na sae ye glinted by
   When I was wi' my dearie.

O, WERT THOU IN THE CAULD BLAST

O, wert thou in the cauld blast
   On yonder lea, on yonder lea,
My plaidie to the angry airt,
   I'd shelter thee, I'd shelter thee ;
Or did misfortune's bitter storms
   Around thee blaw, around thee blaw,
Thy bield should be my bosom,
   To share it a', to share it a'.

Or were I in the wildest waste,
   Sae bleak and bare, sae bleak and bare,
The desert were a paradise,
   If thou wert there, if thou wert there :
Or were I monarch o' the globe,
   Wi' thee to reign, wi' thee to reign,
The brightest jewel in my crown
   Wad be my queen, wad be my queen.

In the autumn of 1795 the poet's health, never very sound, finally broke down, but for months he struggled on, attending to his official duties and all the time growing weaker and weaker. At last he was forced to give in. Hoping to restore his health, he went to Brow, a small watering-place on the Solway, for sea-bathing. The change did not benefit him. The probability of early death was now apparent, and for months it certainly occupied much of his thoughts. During these long months of farewell he presents the melancholy spectacle of a man, whose doom was sealed, being denied the privilege of dying in peace. The war with France had affected British commerce and diminished credit everywhere. During his later years in Dumfries the poet was occasionally in financial straits, accounts were left standing too long unpaid, and sometimes small sums of money had to be borrowed. Nevertheless he always managed to clear his feet, and was perfectly solvent even during his illness and residence at Brow. At his death his affairs were quite in order, and on a balance showed something on the credit side. Nevertheless his breakdown in health caused a heavy drain on his resources, and he had difficulty in at once producing ready cash. As the weeks passed and he kept nearing the ultimate goal, his fears for his family so weighed upon him that he could not always reason calmly. At last the blow fell. A tailor began to demand payment of £7 4s., the price of Burns's Volunteer uniform, and, failing compliance, put the matter into the hands of a lawyer, who wrote threatening a process if the account was not met. In his weak condition this letter threw the poet into a perfect frenzy of fear. At the moment he was unable to pay. All the horrors of the debtors' prison loomed up in his imagination. No doubt he remembered how the last hours of his father's life had been embittered by the same cause. Thoroughly alarmed, he at once wrote two letters imploring financial aid. They bear the same date. The one was to his cousin, James Burnes, Montrose, and asked for £10; the other, to that Thomson to whom he had been sending priceless songs, asked for £5. The letter to Thomson will be read with pathetic interest: "After all my boasted independence curst necessity impels me to implore you for five pounds. A cruel scoundrel of a haberdasher, to whom I owe an account, taking it into his head that I am dying, has commenced a process and will infallibly put me into jail. Do, for God's sake, send me that sum and that by return of post. Forgive me this earnestness; but the horrors of a jail have made me half distracted. I do not ask all this gratuitously; for, upon returning health, I hereby promise and engage to furnish you with five pounds' worth of the neatest song-genius you have seen." Both sums were promptly sent, though Thomson had first to borrow the money. The bank draft from Montrose was not cashed, it being afterwards found among the poet's papers.

There is, happily, a brighter side to this sombre picture. To the outer world Burns presented a bold front, and no one seems to have realised that the dying man was financially embarrassed. He had only to appeal to be answered; but he was too proud to ask. He preserved an heroic silence, he drew a curtain over his miseries save where in his last letters he involuntarily showed his anguish. Those who saw him at Brow seem to have been impressed with his manly fortitude. Mrs. Riddel, an acquaintance whom he had not seen for some time, met him there, and was anxious to show him some kindly attention. Of her interview with the bard she wrote the following affecting account: "I was struck with his appearance on entering the room. His first salutation was, 'Well, madam, have you any commands for the other world?' He spoke of his death without any of the ostentation of philosophy, but with firmness as well as feeling, as an event likely to happen very soon. . . . His anxiety for his family seemed to hang heavy upon him. . . . He said he was well aware his death would create some noise, and that every scrap of his writing would be revived against him to the injury of his future reputation. . . . I had seldom seen his mind greater or more collected."

On July 18, 1796, Burns returned to Dumfries to die. With difficulty he walked up the small hill to his house. His wife, herself ill, was unable to minister to him, and his first act was to write to his father-in-law in Mauchline to send Mrs. Armour to nurse her daughter. But friends of tried constancy tended him to the last—kind Jessie Lewars, for whom he wrote "O, wert thou in the Cauld Blast"; Findlater, his supervisor in the Excise; and Dr. Maxwell, his political associate and fellow-Volunteer. The news that the poet was dying soon spread, and before the dread presence of death all political and personal rancours disappeared. Outside in the streets anxious groups of citizens gathered, eager to know the latest news of their illustrious countryman. They were not long kept in suspense. On July 21 Burns was dead. It is sad to think that he passed away muttering an execration against the man who had threatened him with imprisonment.

After his death Dumfries paid fitting homage to the genius of its great townsman. On the evening of the 25th his remains were removed to the town-hall, and on the following day they were consigned to the earth with much ceremony. His comrades of the Volunteers in solemn parade rendered him all military honours. Two regiments, one of horse and one of foot, lined the streets. The whole body of the citizens participated in the funeral rites. At least ten thousand persons took part in the obsequies. It was no more than his due. And it was a visible manifestation of their belief that one of the great ones of the earth had passed away. But with this tribute, with the pomp and parade and pageantry of woe, with the respectful silence of the throng, the reader cannot help contrasting the misrepresentation, the slander of evil tongues, the cold indifference of society, the petty malevolence of politics, and those last bitter hours.

GLOSSARY

Ae, *one, only*
Aff, *off*
Agley, *off the straight, askew*
Aiblins, *perhaps, possibly*
Airt, *direction*
Ance, *once*
Aught, *eight*

Bear, *barley*
Beets, *fans the flame*
Belyve, *by-and-by*
Ben, *the spence or parlour*
Bickering, *noisy*
Bield, *shelter*
Billie, *good fellow*
Birks, *birches*
Blate, *shamefaced*
Bleeze, *blaze*
Blellum, *idle, talking fellow*
Blink, *a look*
Blinkin', *smirking*
Boddle, a *small coin worth about a farthing*
Bogles, *ghosts*
Bore, *hole*
Big, *to build*
Brae, *hillside*
Braid, *broad*
Braing't, *plunged forward*
Branks, *bridle, a wooden curb*
Brattle, *short race*
Bree, *juice, brew*
Brent new, *brand new*
Burdies, *damsels*
Bure, *bore*
"Bure the gree," *bore off the prize*
Buskit, *dressed*
But, *without*
Byke, *beehive*

Ca', *call, drive "the plough"*
Cannie, *careful, soft, gentle*
Cantrip, *charm, spell*
Carking, *grinding, vexatious*
Carlin, *old woman*
Cartes, *cards*
Chapman, *pedlar*
Chiels, *young fellows*
Chimla, *chimney*
Claes, *clothes*
Cleekit, *linked themselves*
Coft, *bought*
Coila, *Kyles, a district of Ayrshire*
Coof, *fool, ninny*
Cookit, *appeared and disappeared in turn*
Coost, *cast, threw off*
Core, *corps*
Coulter, *ploughshare*
Cour, *to cower*
Cozie, *cosy*
Crack, *talk*
Cranreuch, *hoar frost*
Creeshie, *greasy*
Croon, "gae a croon," *made a lowing sound*
Crummock, *staff with a crooked head*
Cutty, *short, bobtailed*

"Daimen icker in a thrave," *an odd ear of grain in twenty-four sheaves of corn*
Dight, *wipe away*
Dine, *noon*
Donsie, *unlucky, bothersome*
Dool, *grief, sorrow, dole*
Duddies, *garments, rags*

Eldritch, *frightful*

GLOSSARY

Ettle, *attempt*
Eydent, *diligent*

Fairin', *present, reward, deserts*
Feg, *fig*
Fell, *pungent,* "her weel-hained kebbuck, fell"
Fient, *none, not a particle of:* "the fient a pride," *the devil a bit of pride*
Fiere, *chum*
Fit, *foot*
Fittie-lan, *the near horse of the hindmost pair in the plough*
Flichterin', *fluttering*
Fliskit, *fretted*
Fyke, *fuss*
Fyle, *to soil, to dirty*

Gabs, *tongues*
Gar, *to make*
Gar't, *made*
Gaun, *going*
Gear, *wealth, goods*
Glowran, *staring*
Goavan, *dazed*

Ha' Bible, *Hall Bible, so called because it stood in a nobleman's hall*
Haffets, *locks of hair*
Hafflins, *partly*
Hag, *hole in moss or moor*
Hained, *spared*
Halesome, *wholesome*
Hallan, *partition or wall in cottage*
Happer, *hopper of a mill*
Harn, *yarn*
Hawkie, *cow*
Het, *hot*
Hilchin, *halting, prancing*
Histie, *dry, barren*
Hool, *husk of grain, outer skin*
Houlet, *owl*
Hurdies, *hips*

Ilka, *each, every*
Ingle, *fireplace*

Jauk, *to trifle*
Jaukin, *trifling, dallying*

Kail-runt, *cabbage stalk*
Kebbuck, *cheese*
Keek, *look*
Kennin, *a very little, just as much as can be perceived*
Knowe, *hillock*
Kye, *cows*

Laith, *loth*
Laithfu', *bashful*
Lave, *remainder, others*
Lav'rocks, *larks*
Lift, *sky*
Lint, *flax;* "in the bell," *in flower*
Loon, *fellow*
Lowe, *flame*
Lug, *ear, to bring out*
Lyart, *grey, withered*

Maun, *must*
Maut, *malt*
Melder, *meal-grinding*
Mirk, *darkness*

Naig, nag
Nappy, *ale*
Niffer, *exchange*

Outler, *left out at night in the field*

GLOSSARY

Parritch, *porridge*
Pattle, *stick*
Penny-fee, *wages*
Pleugh, *plough*
Plumpit, *plunged*
Poortith, *poverty*

Quean, *young woman*
Quey, *young cow*

Rair, *to roar*
Raxin, *reaching out, elastic-natured*
Reekit, *smoked, smoky*
Rigwoodie, *gallows worthy*
Riskit, *made a noise like the tearing of roots*

Sark, *shirt*
Shaw, *a wood*
Skellum, *worthless fellow*
Skelpin, *walking smartly, resounding*
Slaps, *gates, hedge openings*
Slypet, "an slypet owre," *fallen smoothly over*
Smoor'd, *smothered*
Snool, *cringe*
Soupe, *milk*
Souple, *supple*
Sowth, *to hum or whistle in a low tone*
Spaviet, *spavined*
Spean, *to wean*
Speel, *to climb*
Spier, *to ask*
Splore, *frolic, spree*
Sprittie, *rooty, full of sprits (rushes)*
Stacher, *to walk unsteadily*
Stibble, *stubble*
Stoure, *dust, force of events*
Stowp, *mug or jug*
Sugh, *moan*
Swat, *sweated*
Swats, *new ale*

Tent, *to take heed, mark*
Tentie, *heedful*
Thole, *to suffer*
Tint, *lost*
Tippenny, *twopenny ale*
Towmon, *twelvemonth*

Unco, *strange, very*
Uncos, *adventures, news, out-of-the-ordinary happenings*
Usquebae, *whisky*

Wad, *would, would have*
Wale, *choice*
Wales, *chooses*
Walie, *choice*
Ware't, *spend, use*
Warlocks, *evil spirits*
Weet, *wet, dew, rain*
Wiel, *eddy*
Willyart, *disordered*
Wimplin', *waving, meandering*
Winnock-bunker, *a window seat*